Trains from Grandfather's Attic

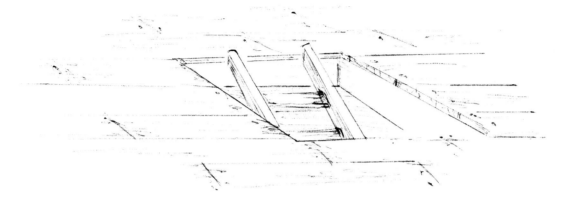

Layout Construction and Operating Techniques for the Prewar Toy Train Enthusiast

by

Peter H. Riddle, Ph.D.

(Diagrams and Photographs by the Author)

Greenberg Publishing Company, Inc.
Sykesville, Maryland

Copyright © 1991
by Greenberg Publishing Company, Inc.

Greenberg Publishing Company, Inc.
7566 Main Street
Sykesville, MD 21784
(301) 795-7447

First Edition

Manufactured in the United States of America

Greenberg Publishing Company, Inc. publishes the world's largest selection of Lionel, American Flyer, LGB, Marx, Ives, and other toy train publications as well as a selection of books on model and prototype railroading, dollhouse building, and collectible toys. For a complete listing of current Greenberg publications, please call 1-800-533-6644 (Fax orders: 414-796-0126) or write to: Kalmbach Publishing, 21027 Crossroads Circle, Waukesha, WI 53187.

Greenberg Shows, Inc. sponsors *Greenberg's Great Train, Dollhouse and Toy Shows*, the world's largest of its kind. The shows feature extravagant operating train layouts, and a display of magnificent dollhouses. The shows also present a huge marketplace of model and toy trains, for HO, N, and Z Scales; Lionel O and Standard Gauges; and S and 1 Gauges; plus layout accessories and railroadiana. It also offers a large selection of dollhouse miniatures and building materials, and collectible toys. Shows are scheduled along the East Coast each year from Massachusetts to Florida. For a list of our current shows please call or write the Maryland address above and request a show brochure.

Greenberg Auctions, a division of Greenberg Shows, Inc., offers nationally advertised auctions of toy trains and toys. Please contact our auction manager at (301) 795-7447 for further information.

ISBN 0-89778-215-1

Library of Congress Cataloging in Publication Data

Riddle, Peter.
    Trains from grandfather's attic : layout construction and
operating techniques for the prewar toy train enthusiast / by Peter
H. Riddle. -- 1st ed.
        p. cm.
    ISBN 0-89778-215-1 : $22.95
    1. Railroads--Models. I. Title.
TF197.R492 1991
625.1'9--dc20   91-25714
                                                        CIP

Table of Contents

Acknowledgements

Neither this book nor my life-long involvement with miniature railroading would have been possible without first the tolerance, then the encouragement, and finally the enthusiastic participation of my wife, **Gay**. She was my severest critic as first reader of this manuscript, and my patient teacher as I struggled with the mysteries of word processing. She has traveled endless miles and waited patiently at countless auctions as I pursued each elusive toy, and her keen eyes and sure instincts have led me to many hidden treasures on train meet tables and in the back recesses of antique shops. Her contribution, like my gratitude, has been unmeasurable.

With their friendship, advice, encouragement and expertise, **Bruce** and **Linda Greenberg** have added much to my education in this field, and to this book. But most important is their dedication to the preservation and expansion of knowledge about this important part of our cultural and technological heritage. Enthusiasts everywhere owe them a great debt. They are fortunate to have contact with many experienced collectors and hobbyists throughout the continent, and one such advisor contributed greatly to this project by reading the entire manuscript: **Cliff Lang** offered many suggestions and corrections, for which I am most grateful.

Through the kindness and persistence of dedicated businessmen-hobbyists, I have been fortunate always to find just the right part needed to salvage my treasures. Chief among these are **George Tebolt**, parts specialist extraordinaire, **Janice Bennett** of Bennett Dry Transfers, **Charles Wood** of Classic Model Trains, and **Ron Leventon**, a specialist in American Flyer.

I would be remiss not to mention **Randy Hill** and the staff at Radio Shack in New Minas, Nova Scotia, for all their help and advice with both my railroad electronics and word processing woes. And **Larry Keddy**, who runs Lark Photographic Services out of Scott's Bay (a lovely spot that is surely one of Nova Scotia's best kept secrets), provided exceptional expertise in preparing my black and white photos.

Through this hobby I have been fortunate to trade with many fine and honorable people, whose generosity, advice and fairness have helped me build a collection of which I am very proud. None has done me greater service than **Tony Hay** of Huntington, West Virginia. His guidance and friendship, when as a newcomer to the hobby I knew next to nothing, helped me to avoid many pitfalls in laying the foundation of my collection.

Two good friends have contributed more than they could know. **Barbara Jordan** is the finest secretary any university administrator could ever hope to work with. I will always be grateful for her quiet competence in managing the affairs of my office in the Acadia University School of Music, allowing me to use my spare time to complete this book. And to **Bob Rushton**, a superb sea captain, dedicated teacher of music and avid gandy dancer, I owe more than I can ever repay.

Peter H. Riddle

July 1991

Several staff members of Greenberg Publishing Company helped to prepare this book for publication. **Barbara Morey** edited the text and developed the book design and layout. **Maureen Crum** designed the cover and offered guidance on the overall design. **Bill Wantz** printed the many black and white photographs. **Donna Price** proofread the manuscript for accuracy and consistency. **Samuel Baum** provided overall support for the project.

Bruce C. Greenberg

July 1991

ONE

The Toy Train as Living History

Antique toy trains are beautiful!
They are also cute, quaint and charming. They are nostalgic and evocative of a simpler era, when learning to do things with one's own hands was a fundamental part of every child's education. Toy trains are sturdy and durable, as witnessed by the huge numbers that have survived decades of hard play and neglect. Equally important, they are works of art, finely crafted examples of the manual and creative skills of inventors and artisans from earlier generations. And they possess one quality that communicates all of these attributes most effectively.

Toy trains are functional!

Produced in 1924 and sold only in Canada, this Dominion Flyer clockwork set was purchased at a country auction, and is almost like new. It was manufactured by American Flyer of Chicago, and is scarce in any condition.

Embodied in their name is the key to their function: they are *trains*, miniature representations of the most revolutionary development in transportation to come out of the 19th century; and they are *toys*, artifacts that were meant to be played with, by children of all ages.

Toy trains should be played with! They are most beautiful when fulfilling their intended purpose.

Collectors delight in discovering, usually in some deeply hidden recess of an attic or at an estate sale, a pristine set of tinplate toy trains in the original box that they came in, unscratched and unrusted, the paint lustrous with the patina of age. (This pleasure was mine when I found the Dominion Flyer clockwork set, which is pictured on the preceding page, on an auction table in Auburn, Nova Scotia, in 1989.)

Yet there is often greater charm to be found in a toy that's slightly dented, somewhat scraped, or even missing a coupler or wheel, for these toys have been enjoyed by their young owners before being stored away. They have been used as they were intended.

Such toys have character, and while their monetary value may be less than the aforementioned little-used set, they have equal potential for bringing hours of satisfaction to a new generation.

Well-worn pickup rollers and chipped paint suggest this tiny Lionel set from the 'teens was thoroughly enjoyed, although not abused, by its young owner.

If you are exploring the hobby of toy train collecting for the first time with this book, consider not just acquiring them, but putting them to their intended purpose. And if you are a seasoned collector but not an operator, try taking a set or two off your neat but static shelves; set up a loop of track, and turn on the juice! The sight of a sixty-year-old toy rounding those three-railed curves can spark a variety of emotions differing greatly from the more passive enjoyment of possessing and cataloging (and inevitably dusting) a wall-mounted accumulation.

You may not wish to fire up your Mint, boxed State Set, or send your 400E Blue Comet careening around the basement floor at breakneck speed. But every seasoned collector has a slightly shabby Lionel 259 stashed away, with a consist of 629 and 630 coaches, or an American Flyer 410-type loco with three or more four-wheeled freights. They make an ideal starting point, with little financial risk, until you have a permanent layout with safeguards against potential damage.

Lionel made thousands of these 259E locomotives, and most can be made to run like new with a little care and attention. These 629-series coaches are the scarce eight-wheel variety, but are not so rare that one need fear an occasional scratch from operating them today.

For the new collector, many operable items are available at fairly reasonable cost. When I first became serious about collecting tinplate, after spending more than three decades in scale model railroading, it seemed as if most of these old toys were either too scarce and expensive or beyond repair. Now I find them almost everywhere, and have discovered that 95 percent of them can be made to look and run like new. Once you begin to look, you'll be surprised how plentiful they are.

I'm about to build my fourth toy train layout in as many years. Come with me and let's get started. Let's climb the stairs and bring down those Trains from Grandfather's Attic.

Why Build a Prewar Layout?

Most operators limit themselves to one of three eras, roughly equivalent to three definable periods in the production of Lionel trains, America's best-known toy train manufacturer. These are usually called *Prewar*, *Postwar* and *MPC* (for Model Products Corporation, the division of General Mills, Inc. that acquired the rights to the Lionel trademark after 1969).

The *Prewar* period includes trains made during all the years prior to 1942, when production was suspended for the duration of the Second World War. *Postwar* trains were made between 1945 and 1969, and best fit most people's mental image of *Toy Train*: they are usually big, colorful Lionels or sleek and slender American Flyers built to a slightly smaller scale.

MPC is a catch-all term applied, sometimes incorrectly, to the production of Lionel trains from 1970 to the present, although the current owner, Lionel Trains, Inc., has no corporate ties to the other conglomerate firms that owned manufacturing rights at various times during the past two decades. The phrase *Modern Era* has recently come into use, and more accurately describes this period of production.

The largest number of operating collectors may be found among the Postwar and Modern Era factions, and many combine both periods, since much of the equipment is mutually compatible. In fact, many of the recently released Lionel items are made from the same dies that were used during the 1940s, '50s and '60s.

These trains are attractive and reliable; most of them perform in a superb manner! And thanks to the collective creative genius to be found among those who worked for Joshua Lionel Cowen and A. C. Gilbert (the manufacturer of American Flyer beginning in 1938), these trains came equipped with features and accessories that kept a young child's boredom (and Father's as well) at bay. These included smoking locomotives, realistic horns and whistles, and automatic

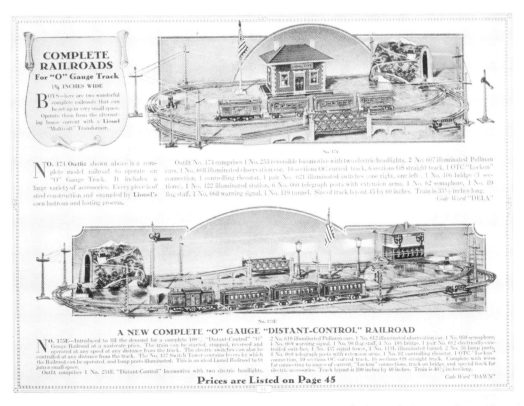

Lionel actively promoted the concept of year-round railroading by marketing train sets complete with accessories and scenery.

couplers. A host of action cars discharged milk cans, dumped coal and logs, corralled cattle and horses, and fired off helicopters and space ships of every description.

It is no wonder that the vast majority of enthusiasts are drawn to this stimulating period of an exciting hobby. Yet the operator of the Prewar era enjoys many of these same delights as well as others, foremost among which is a strong sense of cultural and historical preservation.

Toy trains have always been a seasonal product. Sales during the immediate pre-Christmas period total many times the volume during the remainder of the year, and in many households the 'round-the-tree layout has been the only occasion for displaying these treasures. Manufacturers therefore promoted the concept of building permanent layouts in order to stimulate off-season sales of sets and accessories.

Also promoted, by Lionel especially, was the concept of father-and-son involvement in the hobby. Advertisements pictured family members happily engaged in cooperative layout building, and some ads were so blatant as to suggest that fathers who did not help their children in this activity were neglecting them. One such display suggested, "This father never knew his own son," while a more positive one was headed, "One of the best ways Men get to know each other," picturing Dad and Junior on the floor together.

Whatever the motivation, many layouts were built, and there can be little doubt that many talented scale modelers got their start by following the tinplate route. And in our present age, the construction of a period layout using authentic equipment built in the 'teens, '20s and '30s is a satisfying way to capture and preserve a colorful period of North American life.

Although not everyone will admit it, many collectors probably became involved in this hobby as a means, conscious or otherwise, of preserving their childhood experiences. Many of my own best memories involve the good times I had with my Lionels, and today I choose to spend my leisure hours in a way that makes me happiest. Even more rewarding is the opportunity to share with others the special feelings that these activities evoke. I like to think that by capturing a slice of the past experienced in common with many other boys, I may be able to preserve those good feelings and communicate them to others.

And so the Prewar layout becomes a private museum, and its curator derives considerable satisfaction from helping to keep alive this specialized knowledge of our human heritage. For 20th-century man is a technological animal, and our toys hold up a mirror of ourselves that is startlingly accurate.

This was my first train set, purchased for my older sister for Christmas, 1939, just four days before I was born.

Because of the wonderful mechanical capabilities of these toys, our personal museum should not just provide us with still-life representations. They were meant to operate, and so they should still. The Directors of the Train Collectors Association recognized this need in planning their wonderful public museum in Strasburg, Pennsylvania, where one can see even the rarest trains performing as they did generations ago.

Operating Prewar trains brings special pleasures. Toward the end of the 1930s, manufacturers were just beginning to recognize the depth of appeal to be found in toys that could be

Freight cars that unloaded themselves at the touch of a button exerted a tremendous fascination upon children (and especially their fathers!) when they were first introduced in the mid-1930s. They ejected logs, coal, barrels and packing cases, and there were even accessories that could load them again, all by remote control (see Chapter Ten).

manipulated and controlled in various ways by their young owners. Whistles blew, cars uncoupled, lights flashed, coal dumped, and stations even talked, but only when bidden by the child engineer. As Lionel advertising suggested, many young men would learn in this way to take positive and capable control of their very lives.

Locomotives could be reversed at the touch of a button as early as 1925, thanks to the Ives Corporation's marvelous E-unit. Signals and stations could stop the trains, then restart them automatically, but only when the operator so decreed. And the freight cars seemed almost alive, dumping coal and logs and barrels, or tossing crates of merchandise out on the ground as if a tiny crew were busy inside.

And most of all, the best excuse for building a Prewar layout lies in the very nature of these trains. They are toys, and toys are meant to be played with!

Considerations: What Do You Want in a Layout?

Before beginning a layout, one must decide a number of things in order to choose the proper equipment and to concentrate one's efforts upon the activities that will produce the desired results. There will be almost as many recipes for this as there are modelers.

At my present stage of life, just past the half-century mark, I spend as little time as possible on endeavors that do not please me. I read the books, listen to the music and engage in the activities that I personally enjoy, not those that others or society suggest I should enjoy. For more than twenty-five years as a builder in HO scale, I sifted and glued ballast, placed scale-sized apples on my trees, and endured the frustrations inherent in minuscule parts that looked great but were too small for reliable operation. My eyes were young then; today, neither they nor my nerves can stand the strain!

I am not suggesting that this experience was not generally enjoyable. Scale model railroading provided me with great satisfaction, and my noble but inadequate efforts to emulate the artistry of such modeling geniuses as the late John Allen taught me much.

But now my priorities are different. My current trains are toys, and my first inclination is no longer in the direction of realism, but toward an *impression* of an era. I choose to spend my limited hobby time in ways other than tinkering with couplers, dusting ballast out of switch points and soldering nearly invisible handrails.

Therefore consideration number one for me is that there must be ease of construction and detailing. My roadbed is unballasted; paint gives the illusion of a ballasted track, and allows me to change my layout almost at will, with no glued gravel to scrape off the ties and table top. My trains are toys, and I desire to have the appearance of my layout congruent with their toylike appearance. Therefore my scenery is simple, lightweight and easily changed, and while it would never fool the eye as the magnificent displays in *Model Railroader* magazine do, neither does the time invested in the layout make me hesitate to dismantle it whenever I feel the urge for a change.

And change it I do! The layout I built for display in this book was my fourth yearly effort, and next year I expect it to be replaced by another. Consideration number two requires that I keep the layout as simple as possible while capturing the overall spirit that is intended.

My third intention is also one of simplicity, but this time in the realm of operation. The layout must be designed to function with a minimum of maintenance. When I have a brief half-hour to spare in an evening, I demand that it be spent as I wish; if I desire to watch the trains run, I have no patience with cleaning this, adjusting that and repairing the other before I can hit the throttle.

All of this results in a somewhat bare-bones approach, but one that I hope is attractive. I believe, in fact, that it comes nearest to portraying the type of layout that Lionel illustrated in its Prewar catalogs. But most of all, it is an approach that satisfies me, and I hope that whatever direction you choose to follow in your own layout building, you will find a formula that corresponds with your own philosophy. See color photo 1.

Other limitations are more pragmatic, and foremost among them is space. Since today's homes are smaller than they were at the height of Standard Gauge toy train production, few of us can devote unlimited square footage to the hobby. In any case, there is probably a Murphy's Law somewhere that states, "No train room smaller than the State of Pennsylvania can ever be considered large enough!"

Each of the three popular sizes is roughly twice the size of the next, in ascending order. Lionel's Standard Gauge 1835E towers over an O Gauge 249E, while Mantua's "Belle of the '80's" locomotive from the late 1940s (one of my earliest scale model building efforts) measures less than the height of the big one's drivers.

One's choice of track gauge is largely dictated by the amount of room available. For this and other reasons, O Gauge trains are most often chosen for Prewar layouts. Tight diameter curves (as small as 27 inches), and short cars designed to look good on them, allow for an amazing amount of trackage on a 4' x 8' table. (For proof of this, pick up a copy of Roland LaVoie's latest book, mentioned near the end of this chapter.) Since this size was also the most popular for the majority of the years under discussion, there is still a great variety of equipment available at relatively reasonable prices.

O Gauge trains are also a superior choice in terms of reliability. They are large enough to be sturdy, and can withstand considerable amounts of handling. The smaller gauges that were just beginning to gain popularity during the 1930s were much more delicate, and the relatively unsophisticated technologies applied to their mechanisms made them prone to trouble and sensitive to misuse.

A third factor is visibility. O Gauge trains are a perfect size for viewing, with details large enough for enjoyment without the necessity for magnifying glass scrutiny. However, one should not overlook the advantages of toys made to other proportions, for each gauge has its advantages.

Although the principles to be discussed in the pages that follow can be applied to both larger and smaller sizes, O Gauge was my choice, as it seemed to make the best use of the area I had available to me. My train room must accommodate not only the layout but also my work space and storage. It has been adequate so far, although I must admit contemplating the removal of the wall that divides it from my son's bedroom; maybe someday. . .

The second most popular size for Prewar layouts is probably Standard Gauge, with track 2⅛ inches between the running rails (as contrasted with 1¼ inches for O Gauge). When seen in operation, Standard Gauge trains are magnificent! Their sheer bulk amazes first-time observers; their massiveness and high visibility are most impressive. See color photo 2.

Thanks to clever engineering, these monsters can negotiate fairly tight curves. Conventional track circles in this size measure 42 inches in diameter, allowing for a loop of track on a 4' x 8' plywood board. Standard Gauge layouts often appear crowded, however, as modelers are tempted to cram in every available accessory and lots of trackage. The most effective layouts are those with vast amounts of square footage; observation of the layout at the TCA Museum in Strasburg will support this opinion.

Trains smaller than O Gauge were also made prior to World War II, but in far fewer numbers. The most readily available were OO Gauge and HO Gauge, the first larger by a bit, and both about five-eighths the size of O. These trains represent the beginning of scale model railroading in tiny sizes (scale O Gaugers had been around for a while), and are somewhat removed from the toy category, although Lionel's OO models were available for three-rail track as well as the more realistic two-rail style. Three rails seem to impart a strong toylike impression all by themselves.

The most prominent manufacturer of OO was Scalecraft. Lionel made this size for just a few years, beginning in 1938. Only the firm of A. C. Gilbert (which bought the Chicago-based American Flyer that same year) was well-known for both kit and ready-to-run HO sets before the war. Most other HO trains came only in kit form, and required considerable modeling skill to assemble.

The smaller gauges were not as durable as their larger counterparts, and their performance on the rails was more susceptible to poor electrical contact and adjustment problems. Period trackage, especially the elusive Lionel OO Gauge switches, can be very hard to locate today, and there were few accessories produced to aid in creating a layout.

One other size deserves mention. Toy trains were rarely produced to exact scale prior to the introduction of Lionel's magnificent New York Central Hudson in 1937, but those in O Gauge approximated ¼-inch-to-the-foot, which was close to accurate for the 1¼-inch distance between the rails. Some trains that were designed to run on this track were built to slightly smaller proportions, such as the ³⁄16-inch-to-the-foot O Gauge models by Gilbert's American Flyer and the Louis Marx Company.

After the A. C. Gilbert takeover of the company in 1938, American Flyer's newly introduced models were close to scale proportions, and in fact were converted after the war to S Gauge (two rails, with ⅞ inch between them), which was the correct track width for their size. Marx trains were much more toylike, being produced for the low-priced end of the market and much less substantially built, but were of the same general proportions.

While it is possible to combine these models with regular O Gauge trains on a layout, their smaller size seems somehow wrong (although they can be used very successfully toward the rear of a layout to create a feeling of perspective; see Chapters Three and Twelve). In my opinion, these toys are best run on layouts where they are seen only with their own kind.

The final consideration to be addressed in this chapter is purely a matter of preference: the choice of manufacturer. If availability is the determining factor, Lionel is the obvious answer. Not only did that company sell a vast number of trains and accessories, its superior construction methods and materials have guaranteed a high survival rate. (In Nova Scotia where I live, it is almost the only choice, if one wishes to acquire equipment locally. Only Lionel and Marx penetrated the Maritime Canada market with any great degree of success, and the thin Prewar Marx tinplate is hard to find undamaged and much harder to restore than Lionel's products.)

Next in order of availability is American Flyer O Gauge, which was made in substantial numbers throughout the 1920s and '30s. These have proven to be quite durable; they run well, and original and restoration parts are almost as easy to find as those for Lionel. Some of their features are less reliable (notably reverse units and whistles) since Lionel held superior patents on many technical devices. Nor are there as many interesting Flyer accessories (excepting the wonderful "a-Koostikin" talking station; see Chapter Eleven), but many of them are beautiful and well proportioned, and look great while in operation.

Flyer operators do encounter certain frustrations. The firm seemed to change coupler designs almost at will, and they were mostly incompatible. These included hooks, harpoons, curly-Q knuckles and automatic latches, none of which worked well with the others. (However, Lionel was not blameless in this category either; that firm couldn't decide how far above the rails its couplers should ride, and matching up cars made between 1936 and 1942 isn't always easy.)

American Flyer called its larger line of trains "Wide Gauge" to differentiate from Lionel's use of the label "Standard Gauge." They run on the same size track, however, and for the collector-operator who wishes to specialize in these big toys, the Wide Gauge Flyers have a great advantage over the products of the more famous firm: they are cheaper! While the large Lionels command premium prices at train meets, Flyer's similarly sized products are often quite reasonable.

A third choice, and a personal favorite of mine, would be Ives. This venerable firm (founded in 1868) produced a wide range of trains in No. 1, Standard and O Gauges, most being of high quality and easily restored as excellent runners. Designs range from tiny cast-iron clockwork steamers, pulling coaches less than 6 inches long, to magnificent Standard Gauge behemoths that are classic rarities in this hobby. See color photo 3.

Ives contributed perhaps the most outstanding operational feature to come out of 1920s toy train innovation, the automatic sequence reverse, normally referred to as an E-unit. This ingenious device, powered by a solenoid that functioned at each interruption of track current, rotated a drum which aligned electrical contacts that fed the motor field and brushes, providing forward, neutral and reverse operation with push button ease. No other company could equal this device, and Lionel's imitation was decidedly inferior, a notorious pendulum-operated unit that had no neutral position and frequently sent the locomotive galloping off in the opposite direction at the least break in power.

Ives trains were labor intensive; they required much more hand work to assemble than did Lionel's products. For this and other reasons, the company failed to compete successfully in the marketplace, and declared bankruptcy shortly before the Depression years began. The firm was run jointly by Lionel and American Flyer for a brief period, and then by Lionel alone until 1932, when it was allowed to die. Lionel retained rights to the marvelous Ives E-unit, of course, and soon adapted it for its own line.

In the next chapter the problems of layout design and function will be addressed, but before becoming involved with either building or collecting, one should acquire basic references to serve as aids. There are many model railroad publications on the market, offering advice on every imaginable topic from scenery to wiring to computer-controlled operation. Our special branch of the hobby even has its own excellent magazine, *Classic Toy Trains* (Kalmbach Publishing Company).

Two books also deserve special mention. Roland E. LaVoie has written a comprehensive and immensely readable treatise called *Greenberg's Model Railroading With Lionel Trains* (1989), which addresses nearly every phase of building a toy train layout. Although he deals mostly with Lionel's Postwar period, his techniques are generally adaptable to any equipment, and his clarity of style and practical suggestions make the experience of layout building easy and fun.

The second is called *Greenberg's Repair & Operating Manual: Prewar Lionel Trains*, by John G. Hubbard (1984). The mechanics of these old toys are not difficult to understand, and Mr. Hubbard has explained the principles governing their functions in a concise and understandable manner. He leads the reader step-by-step through the most common repairs to motors, accessories and ancillary devices such as couplers, and his restoration techniques are neither difficult nor expensive; they almost guarantee success. With a little ingenuity, a modeler can also adapt his suggestions to the products of other manufacturers, since their principles of design and electronics are essentially similar.

Each of these texts, and a wealth of others related to collecting, can be obtained from Kalmbach Publishing, 21027 Crossroads Circle, Waukesha, Wisconsin 53187, or from any well-stocked hobby or specialty antique shop. They are a worthwhile investment.

Now let us begin to imagine what our Prewar railroad empire will look like.

TWO

The Purpose behind the Design

Determining what type of layout to design requires first a number of decisions about the purpose behind the proposed layout. This may not be as simple as it sounds. To be both satisfying and enduring, a layout design must be congruent with a modeler's basic likes and dislikes, and the activities he or she most desires to engage in. A little time spent in considering one's motivations in creating this rail empire can prevent disappointment and boredom with the finished product.

One should be prepared for these preferences to change, however, with time and experience. My HO scale model railroads concentrated upon old-time equipment and turn of the century buildings and atmosphere, with little in the way of operation other than moving the trains from point A to point B. When I converted to toy trains and built my first Postwar Lionel layout, my interest focused on the tremendous operating potential of the equipment, as a reaction to my previous efforts.

Switches abounded! All the operating cars and accessories I could afford were crammed into every available space, carefully wired, adjusted and tested until functioning to perfection. And only when the layout was finished did I discover that after a few deliveries of milk cans, a few runs around the horse corral, a few dumped loads of coal, my interest waned. Dust gathered on the log loader and the sawmill, and most of my pleasure came not from the gadgets, but from running the trains.

Layout number two was planned to reflect these new insights. The focus shifted to careful attention to where the trains would go. Hours were devoted to developing traffic patterns for my magnificent Texas Special and Wabash GP-7. Steamer 2065 hauled her freight through a carefully planned series of station stops, with sidings strategically placed and equipped with uncoupling ramps to set out the cars. See color photo 4.

My sleek Union Pacific 2033 streamliner whisked her passengers through sensibly located towns and villages, and my blue 624 C & O switcher had her work cut out for her, sorting the cars into trains for the 2026 Prairies and 675 Pennsy K-4s to haul. As the chief engineer and dispatcher, I could have switched, uncoupled and rearranged for countless hours without ever repeating a move.

And still I found myself spending most of my time happily watching the trains run by themselves.

About this time I acquired the first of my Prewar equipment at an antique auction near Halifax, Nova Scotia's capital city: half a dozen 810-series freight cars and a peacock-and-orange 253 box cab electric with three 607-series passenger cars. All of these trains were scratched and battered, and neither looked right on my layout nor performed well. For several months they sat on the shelf, items of curiosity and no little pride of ownership, but useless from an operating standpoint.

These early 1930s Lionels were the author's first Prewar acquisitions and restoration projects.

One afternoon I decided to attempt to refurbish the passenger set by a little bit of judicious cleaning. I removed the cab from the 253 locomotive, carefully bent back the tabs that secured its number boards and window frames, and took off the headlights and top trim. Assessing the years of accumulated dirt and scratches, I decided that drastic measures were called for, and applied my most powerful all-purpose cleaner.

It did a wonderful job: it took the paint clean off! My ignorance had provided me with a slightly rusted, nearly bare metal shell, and not the slightest idea of the best way to rectify the damage.

For once, reason prevailed over my impetuous nature, and I began to do some research before proceeding further. Magazines and books explained to me the gentle agents I should have used for cleaning the loco. Articles written by experts instructed me on how to prepare the surface, and Mr. Charles Wood of Classic Model Trains supplied me with spray cans of his wonderful paints, in Lionel shades of peacock blue and orange. A little common sense and good luck put the tough old electric motor back in service again.

The results of my first restoration effort look amateurish to me now, but I was immensely pleased at the time. A new phase of my hobby began, and soon the battered 810-series freights were also resplendent in genuine Lionel colors. My hunt for other common and abused trains turned up a considerable number for which reclamation was appropriate, and the roster of shining new-old pieces grew.

The layout, of course, lay neglected. I loved to run these old trains, especially the passenger sets with their interior lights, but with their cumbersome latch couplers and unreliable (or absent) reverse units, they were at their best only when circling a loop.

It was time for layout number three.

Each time I rebuilt my layout, I added extra tables, until the overall square footage shown in the track plan was achieved. With this much space to work with, and armed with this newly acquired knowledge of my inner urgings, I began to liquidate my Postwar items, and sought out Prewar fittings and accessories. The layout was designed for non-stop running, with three continuous loops, a point-to-point run with reverse loops at the ends, and crossover switches connecting each of these main lines with its adjacent neighbor.

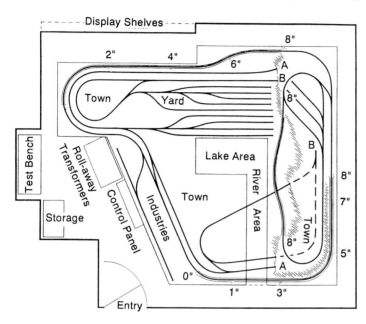

The author's third toy train layout and first Prewar display featured four separate interconnected main lines, and allowed for automatic simultaneous running of six trains.

This, I thought, was the best of all possible worlds. I had provided miles of main line, a complete classification yard and numerous sidings for setting out cars and operating Lionel's four magnificent Prewar action accessories (see Chapter Ten). I could watch the trains run (six at a time, automatically, with hands off the throttles) or route them wherever I saw fit. I had a great time!

And still what I liked best was watching the trains run! The greatest enjoyment came from having them perform for an audience of friends and colleagues, and especially the neighborhood kids.

There could be no doubt; after building three layouts I finally had a layout that satisfied me, a worthy display to show off these amazing toys of years gone by. I knew no greater pleasure than providing each new-found relic with paint and repairs, and placing them on the main line for myself and others to admire.

How could I have ignored Mr. Murphy's Number One Law? Anything that can go wrong, will!

Apropos of all man's best-laid plans, a gremlin or two (or three) infested my perfection. By now the collection had grown to heroic proportions: over forty engines and many times that many cars from a variety of manufacturers. Soon I discovered that Postwar Lionel switches, with their safety-first guardrails, were sure to impede those low-priced American Flyer and Marx locomotives that had gears as large as their drivers. And the tight curves limited my beautiful Flyer Hiawatha to the outside loop, since it needed 40-inch-diameter circles.

Soon I had fine-tuned the trackage so that every train I had could negotiate at least one of the four main lines. But another gremlin soon surfaced. Because Lionel's clever automatic box couplers had not been fully perfected when introduced in the late 1930s, they were prone to release on every stray power rail they touched, especially on the Gargraves and Right-Of-Way switches that looked so good on the layout.

Nor could some other pieces of equipment thread their large Prewar-style wheels through the narrow flangeways of this sophisticated trackwork. Most prone to trouble were my huge 260E steamer and 710-series passenger cars, with their incongruous but factory-supplied Standard Gauge wheels.

With close to four dozen train sets from a variety of manufacturers, each with their own operating peculiarities, far too much time was being spent in setting up each six-train display run. One needed a computer to keep track of which trains could function on which loops. And this was a critical consideration, for I had discovered that I rarely threw the switches and seldom dumped the coal. But I still ran the trains, endlessly around and around the loops, delighting in

Lionel equipped some of its largest O Gauge models, such as this 710 coach, with deep-flanged Standard Gauge wheels. They pass through switches of modern design with difficulty, if at all. Shown at right are an O Gauge wheel set and its Standard Gauge counterpart, for purposes of comparison.

the lights and action. Layout four would have to be designed to provide for continuous, trouble-free running, easy to set up and easy to maintain. That meant fewer switches, of a type that would accept any equipment, and refined trackwork that would be more hospitable to my eclectic collection. I had resolved my personal likes and dislikes, and the next layout would have to meet these needs.

Perhaps the reader can benefit from my experience, and analyze more quickly and easily what type of layout will best suit his or her personality and wishes. One should attempt to determine those aspects of miniature railroading that will provide the most enduring personal satisfaction, and create a design to capitalize on those traits.

For this reason, the concept you will encounter as you progress through these pages reflects my own needs and preferences. There are few switches, and thus fewer risks of trouble on the main line. Although I have included crossovers between all loops, only the straight portions of the switches occur on the main line, thus accommodating equipment needing a broad radius for operation. Except for a few sidings, those switches I have used are Lionel's popular and readily available number 1121, a design without guardrails. (Further discussion of the problems with switches may be found in Chapter Five.)

Any prospective layout builder who wishes to avoid the trial and error approach that I took toward self-understanding would be wise to visit as many layouts as possible before beginning. Fellow train enthusiasts are usually eager to welcome visitors, and by observing and experimenting with the approaches taken by others, one may more easily decide what type of layout to attempt.

Generally these designs will fall into two categories, those created to enhance operation, car sorting, accessory action and switching, and those (like mine) dedicated to trouble-free, hands-off running of lots of trains all at the same time. There are even those true experts who have managed to combine both concepts in one layout!

For those who want the largest possible amount of main line, a layout may be built adjacent to the walls of a room. Such layouts make maximum use of available square footage, but have some disadvantages. First is the matter of access for building and maintenance. If the tables are flush with the wall, all work must be done from the front, and the width of the table is limited by the reach of one's arm. If the entire room is filled with tables, many more access hatches must be built in to allow the modeler to get to all points on the layout.

Another problem is visibility. Many around-the-room designs place the operator and observers in the center. While this may be exciting for the engineer who wishes to be close to the action, it makes it difficult to view the entire set-up at one time. If display running is of major concern, visitors will get the best impression if they can view the entire layout from one edge, all at once. Two of my layouts hugged the walls, but I've found the table-in-the-center method much more pleasing to my eye, and much more attractive to my guests.

For the Socially Inclined: Portable Modular Layouts

In recent years, a trend has developed toward establishing standards for modular layout sections. This concept enables like-minded modelers to gather and combine their modules into layouts of various sizes, limited only by the number of units available and the size of the hall.

An organization called the Tinplate Trackers has established a set of standards for module size, location of tracks and wiring attachment devices. Adherence to these standards ensures the necessary compatibility between members' units. This approach is especially attractive to those collectors for whom the fellowship of our hobby is a major benefit. It also assists those who wish to operate their trains, but have little space of their own for a home railroad.

Who's at the Throttle?

One other concern should be addressed before we proceed to the actual track plan stage: who will be running the trains? If you expect a fair number of young visitors, you must be prepared for them to want to get in on the fun. The average ten-year-old is rarely content just to watch, and sharing the excitement of toy trains with child engineers is a great way to keep us all young.

However, they are unlikely to share your concern for the finer points of safe running. Unless you are prepared to endure the sight of your Flying Yankee streamliner flying off a curve and into the wall, there are certain precautions you might wish to include during the design stage.

Precaution number one is a panic switch; every layout should have a master control that's easy to get to and in plain sight. Cutting off the current has averted impending disaster more than once on my layout.

Second is some type of speed control: several are possible. Curves may be banked, especially on down-grades, to counteract the centrifugal force that can send your prized locomotive four feet straight down onto the concrete. Dangerous curves may be wired to fixed voltage posts, or through resistors, to reduce speed automatically. (You will also want to provide an over-ride switch for use when experienced engineers are at the throttle.)

For the layout featured in this book, I decided to keep the outside loop of track flat on the table. My previous set-up had a 4 percent downgrade on a curve at the very edge of the table, and on one memorable afternoon an eight-year-old with a Casey Jones attitude chose that spot to highball it. Several pounds of American Flyer 3316 steamer made a valiant attempt to punch a new tunnel through my wallboard!

You might also wish to give some thought to accessory location if your younger visitors are as fascinated as mine are with the coal and log loaders. I have a little friend named Heather who loves to make the coal pour out of my Lionel 97 coal tower; unfortunately, she rarely waits for a receptive freight car to be spotted under the spout. It takes some deft work with tweezers and a substantial investment of time to remove a tower full of Lionel coal from among the closely spaced ties of Gargraves track. And I soon discovered that the site of the spill was the least accessible point on the entire railroad!

A final word of warning: there is probably another Murphy's Law that says, "No matter how many safeguards you build into your railroad, some kid will know how to circumvent them." Therefore my final recommendation is to keep those rare cars and locos on the shelf when Junior is at the throttle. The worst disasters always occur when a Blue Comet or Hiawatha is on the track.

Once the basic principles have been established to your satisfaction, it's time to move on to the next phase, track planning.

THREE

Designing the Track Plan

Before we begin to sketch the routes our trains will follow, a few concepts about how we perceive a finished layout should be explored. These principles may, at first reading, seem elementary and obvious, but it is surprising how many otherwise fine layouts have some of their most attractive details unnecessarily obscured, when a little foresight would have prevented such problems from occurring.

Visual Principles

To begin, the train table should be higher off the floor than one might suppose, certainly higher than a desk or a dining room table. I position the front surface 38 inches high; 40 inches would not be too much, although a stool must be provided for tiny visitors. Then the track plan must be designed so that higher elevations climb progressively toward the rear of the layout. This height also allows for sufficient under-table work space.

For this reason, tunnels are most often placed beneath mountains at the back, so that the line of sight is never interrupted. This has an added advantage with relation to perspective: the higher the scenic items (such as mountains) are at the back of the table, the farther away they seem to be.

The modeler should also determine the approximate position of buildings and accessories before the track plan is made final. Placing large buildings and accessories at the front of a layout, and smaller ones toward the rear, creates an artificial feeling of distance and depth. For example, the smallest of Lionel's cute little bungalows were actually built about half the correct size for O Gauge use, and seem out of proportion when seen next to the trains, but putting them as far back as possible adds greatly to the illusion of layout size, and fools the eye as to their actual proportions.

Since the larger accessories are often the most attractive or the most interesting to watch, such as Lionel's massive 117 city station, 164 log loader or 165 crane, their placement near the front of the layout not only adds to creating proper perspective, it also makes it easier to watch them function.

This proud homeowner would have to bend double in order to enter Lionel's half-size houses of the 1930s. Undersized buildings can be quite effective in creating the illusion of distance, however, when placed near the back of a layout.

The control panel should be located so that the engineer has complete visual command of the entire railroad. The reasons are both practical and aesthetic; one must be able to see in order to control, and since watching the trains is perhaps the most enjoyable aspect of operation, the engineer should not have to move away from the throttle at any time just to be able to see. (A discussion of control panel location and design appears in Chapter Six.)

The placement of track with relation to the edges of the table will have considerable impact upon the illusion created. Most model railroaders argue against running the trains parallel to the edge, although I have seen this rule broken with very satisfactory results. In general, prototype rail lines do not follow geometric patterns, and greater realism will result if parallelisms are avoided.

However, if the object of our effort is to maintain adherence to the practices of toy-train empires of the past, geometric patterns of track are desirable. Lionel published in both their catalogs and promotional literature some recommended track plans that were almost always highly symmetrical. Following these guidelines will enhance the period appearance of a layout.

This procedure is easy to follow (in fact almost impossible to avoid) if regulation toy train track is used, as the fixed radii and standardized lengths of track sections will result in patterns with mostly parallel lines or 45-degree tangents. But for the modeler who is willing to compromise by foregoing the authentic appearance of sectional track for the many positive advantages of modern flexible rails, track plan design becomes infinitely more variable and interesting. (The comparative advantages of various types of track are discussed in Chapter Five.)

There is a tendency on the part of first-time layout builders to stuff every available square inch full of track. My early efforts had hardly a spot for a tree to grow! This concept results in an extremely "busy" appearance, which has both advantages and disadvantages. The engineer who loves accessories and lots of action, or who has a limited amount of space, may wish to study the fantastic layout built by Roland LaVoie and frequently shown at Greenberg Shows in the eastern states; it is featured in his book, *Greenberg's Model Railroading With Lionel Trains*. LaVoie's layout is compact, portable, and beautifully executed to provide tremendous variety in a minimum amount of space.

If you have more room, however, there are several reasons to opt for some wide open spaces. Except for urban areas, the real world has a considerable amount of open space (although you might not believe it traveling south on a summer Friday evening on the Garden State Parkway!). Lawns, parks and wooded areas still abound, even in the suburbs, and a visit to my home province of Nova Scotia will show you just how pleasant a really uncrowded place can be! Similarly, a model railroad with "breathing room" presents a much more realistic (and I think pleasing) appearance to the eye.

Another advantage is visibility; too much clutter makes it harder to focus on any one thing. To test this hypothesis, find and examine the display shelves of almost any train collector. Those who place one set of trains on each shelf, with plenty of room at the ends, seem to have much more attractive and interesting displays than those who try to fill every available inch.

How much track is too much? The answer depends upon individual taste, but in recent years I have leaned increasingly toward less and less. While I still love double-tracked main lines with

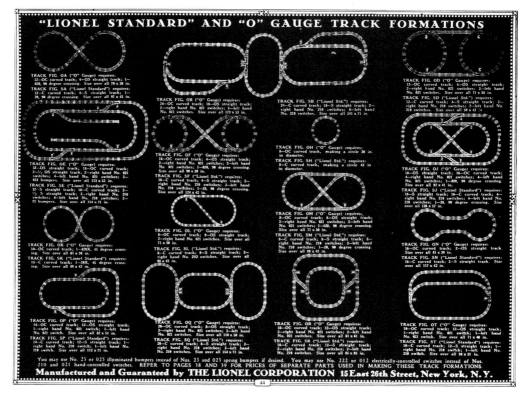

Toy train layouts patterned after the suggestions to be found in Lionel catalogs of the 1920s and '30s exhibit symmetrical characteristics. The use of such track plans helps to preserve the flavor of the era.

crack streamliners racing past each other, their lights flashing in a half-lit room, I no longer include the multiple sidings that once occupied every possibly corner. This means that more of my trains must sit on the shelves instead of on the layout, but I accept this limitation, for now I find I can see them better.

One must also decide what visual effect is desired. My primary enjoyment comes from seeing the trains run, and setting up multiple consists controlled by automatic circuits. As described in the chapters on wiring, the use of such devices as DC relays and automatic-stop stations can create lots of stop-and-go action for six or more trains at once, without the least bit of intervention from the operator. But to be really effective, they must be spread out with lots of running room in between.

My theory is simple: use only two-thirds of the theoretical maximum amount of trackage, and plant some trees in the leftover areas. Including less will allow one to see more!

Planning Ahead for Accessories

When executing the design, take into account the amount of room needed for trackside items. It is often surprising just how much area is taken up by a Lionel 124 or 115 station, and even the smaller 127 variety needs at least 6 full inches between tracks for clearance. And as discussed above, it looks better with more.

Two of Lionel's most popular accessories, the 97 coal loader and the 164 log loader, must be placed between two track routes, as they are loaded from one side and unloaded on the other. I have found that placing the tracks with 15 inches between the center rails makes for the most reliable operation (and the least amount of spilled coal!); this is a lot of room, and must be planned for well in advance.

Lionel's 313 bascule bridge also takes up a lot of room. It measures 21 inches long at the base, with an extra inch and a half overhang at the back, and is almost 10½ inches wide. Adding to the space problem is the need for straight sections of track at either end, as locomotives with long pilots or cars with closely set trucks cannot clear the sides of the bridge if approaching from a curve.

In fact, the problem of clearance is a critical consideration for a number of reasons. Prewar trains were made in a wide variety of sizes, but the wheelbase of each power unit is usually quite small. Lionel's tiny 248 box cab electric measures less than 2½ inches between the centers of the drive wheels. The comparatively huge 251 model has exactly the same wheelbase, but is inches longer, with much more front and rear overhang. See color photo 5.

Toy train curves are sharp, and equipment that overhangs its wheels needs a lot of space to negotiate these turns. Allowance must be made during the planning stages. Since I run fairly large locomotives, such as American Flyer's 4-4-4 box cab No. 3020 and Lionel's massive 263E steamers, I allow a minimum of 4½ inches between the center rails on all curves. Anything less is risking scratched sheet metal, as protruding parts meet car sides in passing.

And while on the subject of clearance, may I suggest never taking anything for granted? Measure and be sure! The first time I sent my newly restored red-and-cream 251 box cab speeding over the rails with its consist of ponderous 710-series coaches, I confidently threw the switch that would take them flashing through the bascule bridge.

They never made it! I can still recall the resounding crunch as the cast headlight tried and failed to pass beneath the bridge's (expletives deleted!) counterweight.

Even Lionel's smaller units can cause problems; the wide cylinder shrouds on the 264E and 265E Commodore Vanderbilts are just one example. On my previous layout, I located one of Lionel's nearly scale 47 crossing gate platforms near the end of a 27-inch-diameter curve. It caused no problems until the day I tested my just-restored Blue Streak 265E on that loop, and caught the edge of the gate base as the Vandy came out of the curve. The result was a 1-inch scratch in the new paint and another fit of bad language! (Why do such accidents never happen to the cheap pieces or the beat-up ones?)

Beware of anything close to the track that projects above the tops of the rails. If in doubt, locate such items well away from curves or back from the track far enough to clear your largest piece of moving equipment. Conduct all tests at slow speed, but remember that rolling a car or locomotive by hand through a suspect area is not enough. When under power, locomotives tend to push toward the outside of a curve, a motion that may not be exactly duplicated by hand pushing.

It is also advisable to plan in advance for access to hidden, blocked or remote areas. Placing several large items side by side near the edge of a table makes it very difficult to reach safely behind them. The result is considerable awkwardness in such tasks as rerailing cars or performing routine maintenance, with the potential for damage to the items in front as you lean or reach over them.

Climbing the Hills

During the Postwar years, Lionel introduced a wonderful feature called *Magnetraction*, whereby magnetized wheels kept locomotives more secure as they rounded curves, and gave them both extra pulling power and added traction as they climbed grades. Prewar equipment had no such advantage, and had to rely on weight alone.

Many of these early locos were quite heavy. This fact assisted them in maintaining adhesion while climbing hills, but also tended to make them careen downgrade at excessive speed. On some models, especially those with heavy castings or weights added under the tops of boilers or cabs, the high center of gravity caused them to be somewhat tipsy on the corners.

When laying out grades, I limit myself to a maximum rise of ½ inch per foot of track, and less at the beginning and end of a slope. This seems to afford even lightweight locomotives enough traction to make the hill, although if you insist on coupling your 810-series freights behind your Lionel Juniors, you might have some trouble!

As a further precaution, I bank inward all curves that occur on grades. A difference as small as an eighth of an inch between the height of the two running rails can be enough to cause the locos to lean inward in a reassuring manner, thus counteracting the considerable centrifugal force they can generate at high speeds.

If your layout features two-way running, the following hint will be of little use. However, if traffic usually goes in the same direction on each of your mains, an additional safety feature can be added. Downgrades may be wired to receive less electrical current automatically, thus slowing the train's descent. This can be accomplished by isolating the power rail on the downhill run, and wiring it through a resistor. Alternatively, one can use a transformer with two throttles (see Chapter Six), reserving one throttle for this separate section.

Some Prewar engines, those with worm-drive gearing, will be less prone to run away down hills, but most locos just love to pick up speed. Reducing the current to the track (and often it must be by a substantial amount) allows the natural friction in the cars' wheels to retard forward progress.

Building in an automatic system to protect downgrades is essential if younger children are among your engineers. During an exciting operating session, it is often impossible to keep track of what they are doing, and you are unlikely to become aware of any difficulty until you hear that fateful crash and find them standing over the crumpled remains of your Hiawatha. (Chapter One contains some other hints for kid-proofing a layout.)

Designating Areas

A final suggestion at this design stage is the concept of designating areas of the layout according to usage. Imagine all those areas that can be reached easily from the control panel as Section A. Section B will be that area which can be viewed easily by observers, without obstruction and close enough for small details to be clear. Section C is the middle ground, and also the largest part of most layouts. It can include either a town or open country, or may hold a classification yard (served by a pop-up access hatch). Section D comprises all the hard-to-see, harder-to-reach spots, such as the back corners and the distant mountain top.

Any equipment needing hands-on operation, such as Lionel's manual 96 coal elevator, should be located in Section A. The operator should avoid having to leave the control panel, and hand-operated accessories that are inconveniently located are usually left to gather dust. Many modelers also locate the yard in this area, if they have one. Derailments are most likely to occur here, and can be corrected without the operator leaving the controls. Whatever its purpose, Section A should never extend more than 3 feet in from the edge of the table, and less if the control panel sticks out into the aisle.

Section B should contain items which need close scrutiny to achieve their desired effect on the viewer. The 165 crane looks most spectacular when placed no more than 4 or 5 feet from the spectator; greater distance diminishes interest. Operating cars, especially those with small items of freight like the 3814 merchandise car that spews out tiny packing cases, must be within easy viewing range, or their magic will be overlooked. And placing uncoupling ramps beyond this range practically guarantees trouble at those spots: Murphy's Law again!

In general, avoid having anything in this area that might need frequent attention. The farther you have to reach to add a drop of oil, or to remove an item with a hidden motor for lubrication, the more you increase the possibility of accidental damage to intervening scenery and equip-

Operating accessories such as this spectacular Lionel lift bridge may be placed anywhere they can be seen easily, but should also be accessible for servicing, either within reach from the table edge or close to a pop-up access hatch.

ment, not to mention the extra investment of time that will be required. My bascule bridge was quite far back on my previous layout, as shown on the plan in Chapter Two. Visually this was not a problem, due to its large size and big motions, but despite the nearby access hatch, it was awkwardly placed when servicing or adjustment was needed, so I moved it closer to the edge of the table.

Stations, of course, can go anywhere, and in fact should be located logically according to where your miniature people most need them. The one exception is American Flyer's a-Koos-tikin, with its internal record player that announces the next train out (see Chapter Eleven). While this gem works anywhere, it isn't loud enough to be heard over the rumble of too many wheels, and placing it up front improves both audibility and the inevitable servicing its complex mechanism requires.

Avoid tall accessories in the middle ground (section C), with the possible exception of light towers or revolving beacons; these are more effective and logical on the mountain tops. Over-sized items draw the eye, and defeat the effects of perspective that add to the illusion of distance. Low-rise buildings, pastures and roadways look fine here; skyscrapers and oil derricks do not.

This leaves Section D, which I reserve for non-specific scenery and my Postwar revolving beacons. (Please forgive me this anachronism; I love the effect of those gently turning red and green lights, and they look just fine with the older toys, too. In fact, I've sneaked a few other Postwar favorites into this layout, as some of the photographs will reveal.) Nothing should be placed here that must be viewed closely, or that needs frequent attention or servicing. While at times it may be necessary to put a turnout or two in out-of-the-way spots (I even have two under the mountain!), gremlins thrive on distance, so be prepared for some uncomfortable moments if you don't provide enough access hatches.

While on the subject of access, I recommend leaving the backs of tunnels open. Trains love to jump the track, or drop essential parts in the furthest, darkest corners, and having to remove scenery or parts of the table framework every time something like this happens can dampen one's enthusiasm for rail travel faster than surly conductors or missed connections. (It also helps if your cat likes to sleep in the tunnels; see Chapter Twelve.)

With these bits of pragmatic philosophy properly reviewed, I offer the track plan on which I based the layout under discussion in the next nine chapters. It isn't perfect (what human creation ever is?) and my next rebuilding effort will, I hope, be even better, but it gave me hours of pleasure in construction, and continues to please me as an animated setting for my collection. In Chapter Four we will address my somewhat unorthodox but practical system of building the tables and generally making the train room a convenient and efficient workplace.

Sharp-eyed readers will notice some discrepancies between this plan and the finished product shown in the photographs that follow. I have purposely not altered the plan after the fact, as changes found to be necessary during the construction process are an inevitable part of model railroading. Additions were also made to the collection during the building process, such as the Lionel Diner shown in several photographs. These items were shoehorned into available spots or used to replace other accessories that appear on the plan, but the overall arrangement of major items is the same as the original conception.

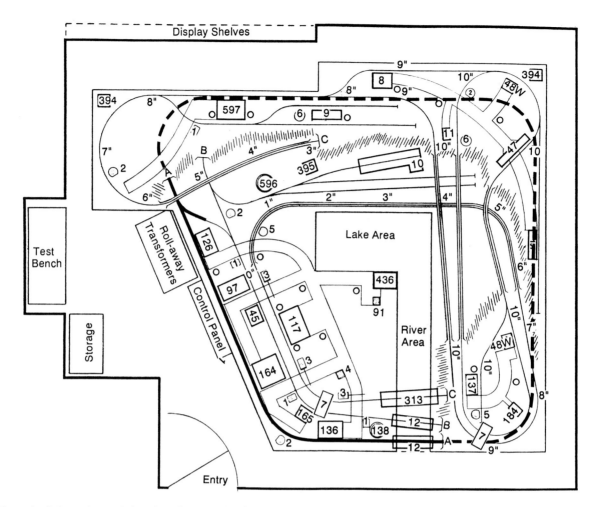

The author's latest layout is based on the principle of continuous automatic operation. It contains four independent loops, each wired for multiple-train running, and joined by crossovers to permit transfer from loop to loop. Nine trains can run at once without attention from the engineer. Most of the accessories are of Lionel manufacture (others are so noted) and were available before the Second World War, with a few exceptions as labeled. Unlabeled circles represent lamp posts of various designs from different manufacturers. Houses and stores are scattered throughout, as described in Chapter Twelve.

The outermost loop of track on the layout is wired to accommodate two trains automatically, when direction of travel is counter-clockwise. The 136 station (lower center) is wired to the track to stop trains when desired. More than half of this loop is concealed beneath the mountain, giving the illusion of trains departing for distant points. Curves have a minimum diameter of 44 inches, allowing large equipment (such as American Flyer's Hiawatha and City of Denver) to operate.

Key to Buildings and Accessories

No. 1	Flashing Highway Signal (Lionel 154 or American Flyer 2206)	
No. 2	Block Signal (Lionel 076 or 153, or American Flyer 2218)	
No. 3	077 or 152 Crossing Gate	
No. 4	57 "Broadway" and "Main Street" Lamp Post	
No. 5	Highway Warning Bell (Lionel 069 or American Flyer 2116)	
No. 6	Water Tower (Lionel 93 or American Flyer 215)	
No. 7	450 Signal Bridge (Postwar)	
No. 8	Industry (wood kit)	
No. 9	Freight Station (metal, manufacturer unknown)	

No. 10	Engine House (wood kit)
No. 11	092 Signal Tower
No. 12	Bridge (Marx 1320, Postwar)
No. 45	Crossing Gateman with Shanty
No. 47	Double Crossing Gate
No. 48W	Whistling Station
No. 91	Circuit Breaker
No. 97	Coal Elevator
No. 117	"Lionel City" Station
No. 126	"Lionelville" Station
No. 136	"Lionelville" Station

No. 137	"Lioneltown" Station
No. 138	Water Tower (Postwar)
No. 157	Freight Station (Postwar)
No. 164	Log Loader
No. 165	Magnetic Crane
No. 184	Bungalow
No. 313	Bascule Bridge
No. 394	Revolving Beacon Tower
No. 395	Floodlight
No. 436	Power Station
No. 596	Water Tower (American Flyer)
No. 597	"a-Koostikin" Talking Station (American Flyer)

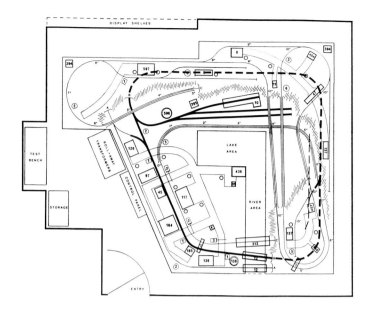

Loop number two is also wired for two trains moving in a clockwise direction. An automatic-stop device detains them briefly in front of the 117 station, and three sidings provide storage space for idle engines and cars. Except for the crossover and the switch leading to the sidings (Lionel 27-inch diameter curve 1121s), no curve is tighter than 34 inches, permitting most O Gauge equipment to run on the main line. The other switches in the yard are Gargraves, restricting this area to locomotives which can pass through their guardrails (see Chapters Two and Five).

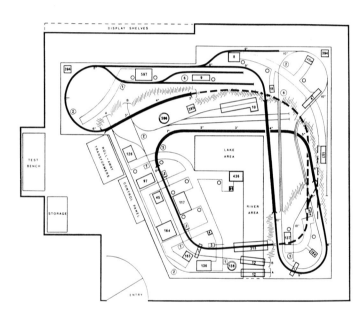

The longest run on the layout is wired for three trains to run simultaneously, and passes over itself on two different levels as it rises to a maximum of 10 inches above the table. Elevation in inches is indicated beside the tracks. Curves are nowhere tighter than 30-inch diameter (again excepting the crossover and sidings), and most locomotives can negotiate them with ease. A hidden crossover (shown beneath the mountain at right) allows transfer of trains to the second loop. The two throttles of a 275-watt ZW transformer are wired separately to the uphill and downhill runs, one to give extra climbing power and the other to retard coasting. Operation is normally counter-clockwise when viewed at the loop at upper left. Because of the complexity of the relay system for protecting three trains, no automatic-stop stations are wired into this loop. However, the protected blocks are arranged to provide the same effect in the area of the 117 station when two or three trains are running.

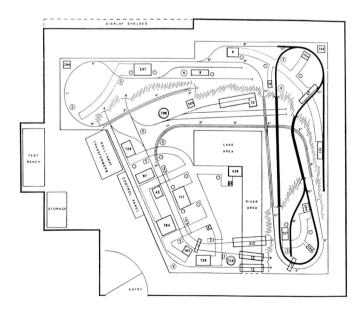

The shortest run has 27-inch diameter curves and two sidings, and is connected to the mountain loop by a crossover siding at the top of the plan. To increase the feeling of perspective, smaller locos and rolling stock are normally operated here, two sets at a time because of the block-protected wiring. The 137 stop station is also wired into the loop to provide the illusion of passengers boarding. Operation is normally counter-clockwise.

FOUR

A Firm Foundation

T he type of table construction used for a model railroad depends largely upon the final surface terrain and the kinds of scenery anticipated. Scale modelers have long favored the L-girder technique developed by the late Linn Westcott, long-time editor of *Model Railroader* magazine. This method involves conventional angle-braced legs which support long beams, each made up from two boards fastened to each other at a 90-degree angle and seen as an "L" from the end. To these beams are fastened variously sized lengths of wood called *risers*, which support the roadbed, scenery and whatever platforms are required for buildings and accessories.

This method allows complete freedom in the creation of hills and valleys. The areas between track and buildings can be raised or sunken with lightweight hard-shell coverings to simulate tiny ponds or great gulches, little hills or even the Matterhorn. This can provide exceptional realism when executed by competent, experienced artists, but it cannot be accomplished quickly. Nor is it easily changed; major modifications usually require a lot of time and create considerable mess. (Those who aspire to create realism in scenery will find a number of excellent books on the subject in any well-stocked hobby shop.)

The average toy train layout from the first half of this century was built on a flat table top, with scenery more often elevated than sunken. This style is much more

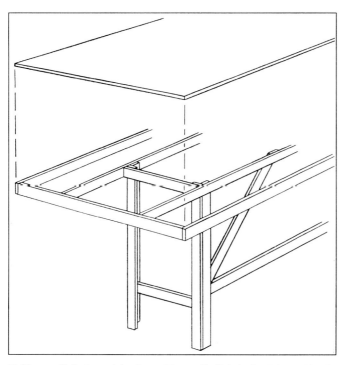

Tables are light in weight, braced but still slightly flexible, and built in standard 4-foot widths and varying lengths.

quickly built, and more easily changed, and while it is not as realistic as rolling terrain (unless you're modeling western Kansas!), the end results can be very satisfying with much less work. And I've introduced a wrinkle that makes rivers and valleys easy to add, without cutting holes in the table. This is described in Chapter Twelve.

The basic construction is simple, and involves only two items from the lumber yard: 4' x 8' plywood sheets, 3/8 inch thick (good one side) and 1" x 3" spruce for the legs and side rails, or runners. The tables are built in modular units, for reasons which will become apparent. All are 4 feet wide (the width of the plywood sheets), and vary in length from a full 8 feet down to 2, as shown in the accompanying diagram.

The tops are glued to the runners, and held in place while drying with finishing nails on 6-inch centers. Cross braces add stability, but allow sufficient flexibility to accommodate slightly uneven floors. They are rigid enough for firm support, yet are still light enough for one person to handle. (Since my son moved to Vancouver, I have to do all my lifting alone!)

The leg supports are also simple and light. Two pieces of 1" x 3" lumber 375/8 inches in length are glued and screwed (or nailed) at a right angle, in an "L" shape when viewed from the end. Placed below the 3/8-inch top, they provide an overall height of 38 inches. Braces are added between the legs at 90-degree angles, and between the legs and the tables at 45-degree angles, as shown in the diagram. Braces are always placed in two directions to ensure stability, parallel to both the length and the width of the table.

The woodworking techniques involved are not complex, but if one is inexperienced in this area, it would be wise to pick up a good text on the subject, or to enlist the aid of a skilled friend. Using a carpenter's square, be sure that all legs are at exact right angles to the table tops, and that they are securely fastened to the side runners, rather than to the plywood tops; this will prevent buckling under load.

The tables may now be joined according to the needs of the overall track plan. The diagram shows the various sizes of tables on my layout, and how they fit together to accommodate the planned scenic details and the access hatch. The empty spaces that result will later be filled with a river and lake. Note that this method avoids the necessity for cutting the table for any below-ground details. Furthermore, when the modeler decides to change the plan at some later date, the tables can be rearranged in another pattern, and lake holes will not have to be filled in.

Critics may point out that this plan is unnecessarily complex, and that a lesser number of larger tables would have achieved the same purpose. This is true, and had this been my first layout, fewer tables would have been used. But this design incorporates all of the table sizes used in an earlier smaller layout, and I saw no reason not to use them. That is the beauty of this method for restless souls like me who change things frequently: it can be adapted to new shapes with a minimum of work.

Note that one of the tables is triangular, rather than the standard 4-foot-wide modular size. This accommodates the unusual shape of my train room, providing space for my work area and room for observers. It allows me to make optimum use of the space

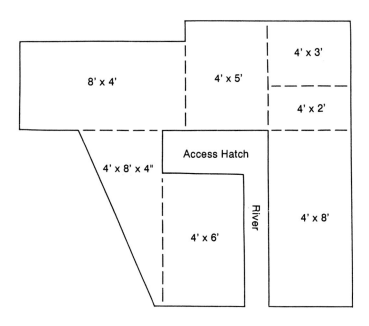

Each of the table sizes was planned to fit into this overall jigsaw puzzle, providing a completed table with room for the river and lake (which also forms an access hatch) incorporated without the need for sawing holes.

Bolts secure the tables from below, and are easily removed if the tables are to be rearranged. The location of the holes is not critical; if the tables are later joined in a new pattern, new holes may be drilled as needed.

available in this unique situation, but most rooms will need nothing more than rectangles.

The tables are joined with 2-inch stove bolts, as shown in the photograph. Clamps are used to align the tables with their tops exactly even, and ¼-inch holes are drilled through the adjacent runners every foot or sixteen inches. The bolts are inserted and secured with washers and nuts. It is recommended that washers be used beneath the bolt heads as well as the nuts to avoid unnecessary penetration of the soft spruce runners.

If the modeler is reasonably agile and not built to National Basketball Association specifications, working beneath these tables will not be difficult. The 38-inch height allows sufficient headroom when wiring from below, but is not so great as to cause arm fatigue when working overhead. My height (5'11") is close to average, and I find myself comfortable performing most under-table operations when sitting on the floor.

This calls to mind a special consideration if you are planning a new home in the near future. Most model railroads are located in a basement or garage, which normally have concrete floors. Insulate the underside of the floor thoroughly before it is poured, and working on the layout will be a lot more comfortable as a result. No matter how efficient your heating system, it cannot compensate for the bone-chilling transfer of caloric energy from hindquarters to uninsulated concrete! (If you're stuck with a cold floor, sit on a cushion or heating pad; it's inconvenient to move around all the time, but better than terminal posterior frostbite.)

While on the subject of temperature, it would be wise to invest in zoned heating if you are planning a new home or rebuilding an old one. The average degree setting for a room differs according to the activity level therein; people prefer higher temperatures when sitting and reading, as opposed to being involved in a rousing game of ping-pong, and working on the layout falls somewhere in between. It is also nice to be able to provide comfort for visitors, and since the average basement is cooler than upstairs, zoned heating allows warming one area without overheating others. (I first became aware of this factor when I noticed that one frequent visitor never removed his parka and mukluks when running the trains.)

Closely related to this is humidity control. The relative level of moisture in the air has almost as great an effect on comfort as temperature; between 45 and 55 percent is ideal. A hygrometer for measuring humidity is an essential tool for the toy train collector for another reason. When my wife first noticed tiny flecks of rust on the wheels of several prized cars, I had to come to terms with the dampness that is inherent in even the best-designed basements in our Maritime Provinces climate. A couple of hundred dollars invested in a dehumidifier is a minor expense compared with the potential damage to tinplate toys that rust represents.

Returning to the main topic, the modular table design also allows for spacious working conditions below decks, provided one has not gone overboard on the number of braces. (There is nothing like a repeatedly bashed forehead to convince one that a single brace in each of two directions is sufficient for lateral stability.) Try to plan ahead for working corridors radiating outward from the control panel area, as most of the movement underneath the layout involves running or tracing wires.

My layout needed only one access hatch, measuring 2 feet wide by slightly over 5 feet long, to allow me to reach any point with relative ease. Performing delicate or complicated tasks at arm's length is tiring, and being able to approach any problem from two opposing angles makes everything much easier. A table that can be reached from one side only should never exceed 4 feet wide, and even then a chair may be needed to allow one to lean over and work at the back. I prefer a maximum of 3 feet, and a 6-foot width for areas accessible from both sides.

Before moving on to the infinitely more interesting phases of building our railroad, the topic of lighting should be addressed. To paraphrase a famous quote, you can never be too rich or too thin or have too much light on a model railroad. I prefer adjustable track lighting for this purpose, using removable heads that can be swiveled 360 degrees. This allows light to be directed wherever it is needed, and also provides for special effects, such as sunrises, when the urge to photograph your masterpiece occurs.

Track lighting with bulb housings that swivel will allow illumination to be directed wherever needed. Three or more housings may be mounted on each track, and the average 15-amp room circuit can easily accommodate a dozen or more in addition to the layout's transformers.

Track lighting allows for easy selective illumination by flooding certain areas to focus observers' attention, highlighting a centerpiece display, eliminating shadows in an area to be photographed, or providing extra light where needed for building and maintenance chores. It also allows a bit of cost control, when compared with systems where all lighting is activated by a single switch. Being able to energize only those lamps which are specifically needed definitely saves on the power bill. (Every time I fire up my bank of transformers and set the floods for high noon, the Nova Scotia Power Corporation declares a dividend!)

We're almost ready to put down some track, after we've decided what kind to use. But first, cover the entire surface of the layout with a neutral tan color. I use latex paint with a semi-gloss surface; flat paint looks a little better, but is much harder to keep clean, and glossy finishes, while easily washable, look highly artificial. Latex paint is less durable than oil-base, but much easier to clean up (as I discovered the day the cat tipped half a quart over on the carpet!), and since the life span of each of my layouts is about twelve months, I don't need the lasting qualities of the Mona Lisa.

As described in Chapter One, sifted gravel ballast and similar flights into realism may be fine for some, but require too much of my time in return for the satisfaction they bring. I am building a toy train layout, not a scale model railroad, and the overall impression I am seeking is one of simplicity and suggestion, rather than miniature reality. In Chapter Twelve we will discover how this tan base coat provides instant roadbeds, footpaths and dirt areas, easily and conveniently.

Now we must choose the track!

FIVE

Trackwork ~ Authentic or Practical?

S ectional toy train track dates back to around the turn of the century, when some European manufacturers and the Ives Corporation in the United States first included it in their train sets. It endures to this day, and in fact modern products will mate with O Gauge track produced many decades ago. The smaller HO and N Gauge train sets also use this sectional approach, as did American Flyer's S Gauge, dating from the mid-1940s. The situation is the same for Standard Gauge.

In general, O Gauge track comes in two different forms, distinguished mostly by weight and rail height. The more substantial style has heavy formed-metal ties and thicker rail, and measures ⅝ inch from base to rail top. Lionel's version, introduced in 1916 and still used today, was curved to make a circle approximately 31 inches in diameter, while American Flyer's product formed a 40-inch circle.

The lightweight version has smaller rectangular ties, and measures only ½ inch to the top of the rails. It is made of thinner metal, and is less durable. It had its genesis in the clockwork sets of the Ives Corporation; this firm simply added a third rail when it began to market electrically powered trains. Because of the 27-inch-diameter circle it forms, this track is usually referred to as "O-27", or simply "O27".

Both types of track have a gauge (distance between the running rails) of 1¼ inches, and theoretically all O Gauge equipment made by any manufacturer can run on either the heavy or the light style. This is true for straight sections, but some larger engines cannot negotiate the tight

The regular O Gauge track on the left is more substantially built and ⅛ inch higher than the O27 version beside it. Note especially the curved bases of the larger ties, and the larger diameter of the rail head on the O Gauge track.

O27 curves, a factor which must be considered by modelers who plan to operate with sectional track.

By the mid-1930s, manufacturers were beginning to move away from the toy look in favor of more realistic trains. Locomotives grew longer, and models of the newest prototype streamliners were introduced, some of them nearly to scale in length. Because these trains could not operate on small-radius track, Lionel introduced its wide-radius O72 line with the new Union Pacific and Hiawatha sets. This track measured 72 inches over the diameter of a circle, and required space in the home even greater than had the 42-inch-diameter curves of Standard Gauge sets. A 6-foot circle takes a lot of floor space!

American Flyer compromised. Its 40-inch circles were already larger than the regular Lionel curved track, and their newer, longer models were modified to negotiate these curves, not always with the greatest success. Their first model of the 4-4-2 prototype Hiawatha appeared to have a four-wheel pilot truck. However, only the front pair of wheels swiveled. The rearmost pair of pilot wheels was actually mounted on the main frame with the drivers, making the wheelbase very long. Because the first and second sets of pilot wheels were different sizes, this model looked unbalanced and did not run well, and the following year a fully turning four-wheel pilot truck was substituted. While this system resulted in better tracking, 40-inch-diameter track was still necessary to keep it on the rails.

In the earliest version of American Flyer's Hiawatha locomotive, introduced in 1936, the front set of pilot wheels turned, while the back set was rigidly affixed to the chassis. Its performance on the rails was less than spectacular, and Flyer changed the design the following year so that all four pilot wheels swiveled.

It is interesting to note that while the trailing truck on this locomotive appears to have four wheels (unlike the prototype, which was a 4-4-2 Atlantic type), there are actually only two; the forward journal on each side is a dummy. (Lionel Hiawathas were more accurate, with a realistic-looking two-wheeled trailing truck.) Since this same system was also used on Flyer's earliest Hudsons, it is speculated that the truck was used on the Hiawatha for reasons of economy, as the same parts could be used for both locomotives, although when the Hudson

The trailing truck on Flyer's Hiawatha appeared at first glance to have four wheels, but only the rear journal actually covered an axle. Since there was no hole punched in the side frame for mounting a front axle, and the prototype had a two-wheel trailer, it is assumed that the manufacturer did not consider this inaccuracy to be of substantial importance.

received a true four-wheeled truck in its second year, the Hiawatha retained the incorrect-looking one.

Many American Flyer locomotives from the 1920s and early '30s came with lightweight 27-inch-diameter track, and will work well on these curves. The smaller units look fine, but Flyer's graceful 3302-type locos and slender 9½ inch freight cars appear awkward in such close quarters; they deserve more space.

All Ives trains could negotiate the O27-style track, and when Lionel eventually gained complete control of this firm, it adopted the lighter trackage for its low-priced Lionel Junior line, later renamed simply *O27* to distinguish them from the more expensive offerings, known as *O*. Louis Marx also adopted O27 for his line of low-priced offerings.

By 1936 the situation was this: American Flyer trains came with 40-inch-diameter track of the heavier type, and Lionel offered three options according to price and model, light O27 for the low-cost sets, heavier O (31-inch-diameter) for the regular line, and O72 for the long streamliners. To complicate matters further, the latter firm's introduction of the magnificent scale Hudson in 1937 was accompanied by a complex system of realistic track with a prototypical T-head design, giving Lionel four styles. Only O and O72 could be combined without modification, as the O27 pieces were too low and their mating pins too thin for proper connection to the larger sizes. The T-rail track used a completely different system of assembly, requiring a special wrench to tighten nuts on connecting fishplates between each section.

American Flyer briefly marketed an odd-ball variation that had a fourth rail and fiber tie base, which was used for whistle blowing. Lionel held the patent on a DC-operated relay for blowing its tender-mounted whistles, so when Flyer put this option in its trains, a different system was needed. They fed current to the whistle motor via a Y-shaped pickup shoe that contacted the fourth rail.

American Flyer's whistle-blowing system used a fourth rail which supplied current through a special contact shoe mounted on a tender or streamliner truck, as shown here beneath a 1936 Burlington Zephyr baggage car.

This track was extremely expensive to produce, and it looked horrible, even less like real railroad tracks than the three-rail variety. The company abandoned this option after only one year, and moved its whistle into a trackside billboard unit. As long as an engineer blew the whistle when the train passed near the billboard, the proper effect was achieved, although Lionel's on-board whistle was much more practical. (Flyer did have a mechanically driven whistle in some of its low-priced locos, but the constant on-and-off sequence was unrealistic, and could drive you crazy; see Chapter Seven for details.)

Used track is readily available at reasonable prices (I have a basement full of it if anyone needs some!), and usually a little cleaning is all that is needed to make it useful again. However, it takes a lot of work to restore the shine of newness, and the modeler who wants pristine trackwork can invest in modern reproductions, which look very little different from originals. Lionel still makes it, as do several specialty firms and K-Line; their advertisements may be found in such magazines as *Railroad Model Craftsman, O Gauge Railroading, Classic Toy Trains* and *Model Railroader.*

Sectional track poses certain inherent problems for the operating layout. Its electrical continuity depends upon the mechanical connection between its male pins and female rail ends. Although a tight fit ensures good contact initially, the vibration of the trains and natural oxidation of the metal causes voltage drops to develop, making the trains run more slowly at certain points on the layout.

The most common method of avoiding this involves soldering bridge wires across each junction, a time-consuming process that also makes changing the layout at a later date much more difficult. An easier but less positive fix is the provision of extra feeder wires to carry current to distant points, but unless a lot of supplementary feeders are used, voltage drops will still occur.

Another problem is the design limitation imposed by fixed-radius curves. Although several different sizes are available, including diameters of 27, 30, and 33 inches (formerly produced by Marx and no longer made), and 42, 54, and 72 inches, sectional track imparts a geometric, square-cornered appearance that is decidedly toylike, but does not make optimum use of space. Nor does it allow transition curves. Real railroads, and the better scale models, never build their curves with a constant radius. Instead, they begin their curves gradually, decreasing the radius as the curve progresses, and ease into the next straight section little by little.

Toy train track does not allow for this; our miniature locomotives plow into the turns and whip out of them with what must be head-snapping effects on their tiny passengers, as well as plenty of friction in their mechanisms. Visit a good scale model layout with transition curves and watch the action for awhile; the difference will soon become apparent.

The heavier O Gauge track is a better choice than O27 for durability, but its oversize appearance is less pleasing to the eye. The proportions of O27 are closer to scale, but these lightweights deform more easily under the constant pounding of the rolling stock, and need more maintenance.

Finally, sectional track has one additional electrical disadvantage: its grounded running rails are connected together by the ties. The Lionel Corporation recognized very early that by simply insulating one of the running rails and connecting it directly to an operating accessory, the circuit could be completed when any set of wheels entered that section. Current was passed from the ground rail through the axle to the insulated rail, and thence to the crossing gate, bell or gateman.

Gargraves (top) and Lionel O Gauge track.

This system is far superior to pressure-activated circuits (such as Lionel began to use just before the war), but modifying the track sections is a fussy job involving bending the tie flanges and inserting fiber spacers. Lionel has not sold ready-made insulated sections for many years, but the modern alternative described below has this feature built in.

The foregoing observations were my justification for using flexible trackage, thus abandoning the "toy" look on my period layout. The advantages were simply too great to ignore.

The Practical Alternative: Flexible Trackage

Gargraves Phantom-Line trackage has been on the market for many years. It consists of realistic T-shaped rails inserted into stained wood ties, and comes in 3-foot lengths. The center rail is black and therefore slightly less obvious than a shiny one (although the firm also makes this product with three bright rails, minus the "Phantom" label).

All three rails are electrically independent, a feature that allows a number of clever electrical tricks (including triggering gates, bells and lights) without modifying the track, as described in the next chapter. While practice and patience are necessary to avoid kinking, it can be curved to the 27-inch diameter equivalent to O27 sectional track or larger. Even smaller radii are possible, although only the smallest locos can negotiate such sharp curves, and they don't look good doing it. Transition curves are easily made.

Some cutting is necessary, as the outer rail on a curve will be shorter after bending than the other two, the innermost rail becoming longest of all. A razor saw or rail nippers will make the task easy. These sections can be secured to the table top without difficulty. While sectional track has holes provided in the ties to accommodate screws, Gargraves track allows the modeler to fasten down any tie, as they are relatively soft and easily drilled. Failure to pre-drill the holes, however, will usually result in split ties. (And while on this subject, nails should never be used to fasten track; they are impossible to remove neatly when changes are desired.)

The smallest possible screws should be used. My preference is for ½" x #4 screws, as they need not be held in place when started, but cling to the end of the screwdriver, allowing the modeler to hold the track with the other hand. I drive about a hundred at a time into a scrap board and spray the heads black before using them; it makes them almost invisible when installed.

The longer track sections improve electrical continuity, and I make it a practice to run a feeder wire to every piece of track, as described in Chapter Six. This has banished voltage drop on my layout, a problem that is much harder to control with sectional track.

The biggest advantage of using flexible track, of course, is complete freedom of layout design. Curves may be gentle or tight, and sidings may be eased into spots that would be impossible with the fixed limitations imposed by regular toy train track. The appearance is also excellent. While modelers often add additional wooden ties beneath sectional track to gain a more realistic appearance, they must be made very wide in order to match the metal ties, and hardly look real. Gargraves ties are better proportioned.

It is possible to combine flexible track with regular O or O27 sections, despite the difference in rail shape. Gargraves sections are joined by flat brass pins, but the firm makes two sizes of white metal transitional pins that fit Gargraves rails on one side and either O or O27 rails on the other. A word of caution is in order: these pins do not tolerate much bending, and will break off in the center if flexed unduly. An eighth-inch shim under the ties is needed to match Gargraves rail height with O Gauge; O27 matches exactly.

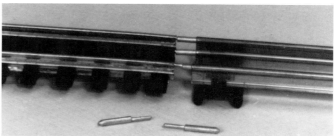

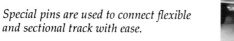

Special pins are used to connect flexible and sectional track with ease.

Switches and Their Problems

Most model railroads contain at least some switches to provide trains with alternative routes of travel. No accessory is more basic to railroading action, yet none is more likely to cause operating difficulties than these ingenious and varied devices.

Many different designs have been tried. Scale modelers use efficient switches (they call them by the more accurate name of *turnouts*) that approximate the real thing, but toy train operators are plagued by the presence of that power-carrying third rail, which causes complications.

The earliest examples are suitable only for locomotives made during that same period. Pickup rollers tend to drop into large gaps between their rails with a jolt, sometimes breaking, and derailments are frequent because of the crude tolerances used in construction. They give a nice antique appearance to the layout, but not much peace of mind to the operator. Both automatic and manual versions were made.

The earlier switch designs, such as this wye of European origin and Lionel's common O Gauge unit, are unreliable in operation. The Lionels were certainly attractive, however.

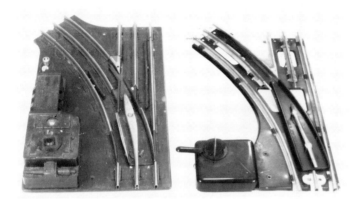

In the switch design at left, the rails at the frog are fixed and do not move. The points may be moved either to the right or left to direct the wheels of the locomotive and cars. Note that this design requires guardrails on either side of the frog to ensure proper tracking. In the other design, both curved and straight running rails rotate together. This action aligns the running rails in a continuous or closed frog, eliminating the need for guardrails.

O Gauge switches follow one of two basic designs. Either they have a fixed frog and movable points, as demonstrated by the Lionel 1122 on the left side of the photo, or they have swivel rails that align both frog and points at once, as shown by the Marx switch on the right. (The *frog* is that place where the innermost straight and curved rails intersect; the *points* are the movable ends of the rails which send the locomotive in the desired direction.)

Most Prewar switches follow the fixed-frog design, and have guardrails as shown in the photograph. This poses no problems for the majority of locomotives, but there are a few that cannot pass through these switches. Some low-priced American Flyer and Marx engines had gears built into the drive wheels that extended all the way to the edge of the wheel flange. Such wheels are unusually wide, and get stuck in or ride up over guardrails, with a bouncing motion that sometimes causes derailments.

To avoid problems, both Marx and American Flyer used the closed-frog approach to switch design. Modelers who have in their collections locos with large wheel gears may wish to use only these switches. Flyer models are the same height as and mate with other brands of O Gauge track such as Lionel, but they are curved to a 40-inch diameter, which does not work well with standard 31-inch O Gauge track in conventional layout designs.

Some low-priced locomotives from Marx and American Flyer may have thick drive wheels with cast-in gears. These cannot pass through switches with guardrails.

Marx switches have the same curvature as O27 track made by other manufacturers, and are built to the same dimensions of height and rail-joiner (track pin) thickness. However, the products of this manufacturer were targeted at the most economical end of the market, and are of minimum quality and dependability.

Lionel's magnificent 022 O Gauge switches (built from the mid-'30s to the present), which are sturdy and reliable, have guardrails that trip up the Flyer and Marx engines. However, Lionel also manufactured an automatic O27 switch beginning in the mid-1930s that used swiveling rails and had no guardrails: the 1121 design. These dependable switches were made in large quantities both before and after the war, are easy to repair, and will pass the wheels of every manufacturer's O Gauge locomotives. As an added bonus, they mate with Gargraves track without modification.

Made in huge quantities and having no guardrails to catch the large gears on some locomotives, Lionel's 1121 switches in O27 Gauge are an almost ideal choice for the operator who runs equipment from many manufacturers. Their only drawback is a tight 27-inch-diameter curvature.

For this reason I use 1121 switches for all applications where those tricky locomotives will be run. I even include them on main lines where I run locomotives (such as Flyer's Hiawatha) that cannot negotiate O27 curves. I simply ensure that the straight portion of each switch is on the main line, and never turn them when large locos will be passing through.

Gargraves makes switches to match their track, mounted on plastic tie bases and very reasonably priced. Right-Of-Way Industries and Ross Custom Switches market a similar type in a much higher price range, but for the difference in price the modeler gets wooden ties, hand-made quality and a wide variety of types, from wyes to complete yard sets. I have used both brands successfully with Postwar equipment, but Prewar trains can encounter some problems when negotiating these switches.

Before World War II, toy trains were made with oversized wheels with a lot of play in the trucks and axles. The pilot and trailing wheels on most American Flyer locomotives, for example, had very wide treads and thick, deep flanges. Since modern switches are made to close tolerances, Prewar wheels frequently brush

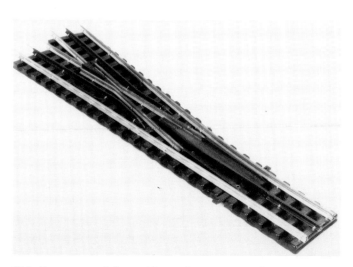

This Gargraves switch provides good appearance at low cost, but the wide third rail can cause short circuits with oversized Prewar wheels, and the guardrails impede locomotives with gears the same size as the drivers.

against the third rails and guardrails, causing short circuits. In addition, the guardrails prevent passage of locomotives with large gears attached to their drivers.

Some of these problems can be overcome, and I like to use Gargraves type switches in yards; they allow sidings to be placed much more closely together than Lionel's designs. I have had reasonable success in preventing shorts by painting the offending edges of the third rails with polyurethane, available in hardware stores as a substitute for varnish. This substance is very hard, and several coats ensure insulation between the rail and any wheel that may touch it from the side. Care must be taken to avoid getting the urethane on the top surfaces of the rails, and it must be allowed to dry completely before use.

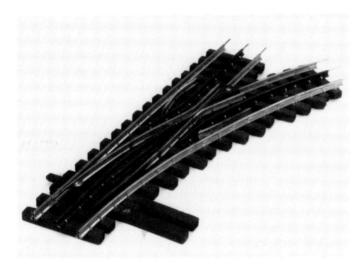

These well-made products of Right-Of-Way Industries are not recommended by the manufacturer for use with Prewar trains, but may be modified successfully by insulating the sides of the center power rails with urethane or even electrical tape. Some cars and locomotives may still cause short circuits, however, but the wide variety of types and radii that are available may make fussing with them worth the trouble.

Difficulties may still arise. The pickup rollers on early whistle tenders and lighted passenger cars are more flexible than those on their Postwar counterparts. Sometimes they bridge the gap between the running and third rails of switches, and may even be displaced from the third rail enough to cause side pressure on the trucks and subsequent derailments. It takes some precision tinkering with these rollers to keep them in line.

Momentary shorts are not too serious, although the sparking that is seen when the cars pass through the switches is not desirable, and leaves deposits on the rails. If the trains travel at slow speeds, however, or stop over a switch, such short circuits may interrupt the current long enough to stall the engine.

The biggest attraction of Right-Of-Way or Ross Custom switches is the wide variety of radii available, making custom track plans feasible. If one is willing to trouble-shoot until they are modified to accept all of the varied equipment in use on a Prewar layout, they provide a very realistic appearance.

A few conclusions are in order, from which one may choose according to personal needs. If you are running Lionel equipment alone, use Lionel switches. If you run only smaller equipment from different manufacturers, use switches without guardrails (Marx, Lionel 1121). If you mix longer equipment with models that have protruding gears, use American Flyer's 40-inch-diameter switches of closed frog design. These can even be mated with flexible track, by shimming up the latter to the same height. If you run Lionel's O72 models (Hiawatha, Union Pacific, Rail Chief), that firm's O72 switches (wide-radius versions of the 022 model) are a good but expensive choice, as are the wider-radius products of Right-Of-Way Industries.

And if all of this is too confusing or seems to be too much trouble, use no switches at all, and run your trains on concentric loops. There's no better way to guarantee trouble-free operation.

Uncoupling Ramps

Both of the major American toy train manufacturers introduced automatic uncoupling shortly before the war, Lionel in 1938 and American Flyer in 1939. Flyer's design was a simple mechanical device that survived well into the 1950s on their S Gauge products. It consisted of a cast latch with a notch on the underside that rode up on a pin extending from the side of the coupler on an adjacent car, then dropped down over that pin to couple.

American Flyer automatic couplers were simple pivoting latches that mated with pins on connected cars.

The uncoupling ramp consisted of two simple metal blades that protruded between the rails. Pressing the coupler activator caused the blades to rise, pushing the coupler pins out of the notches and separating the cars. For today's operator, this mechanism is simple and reliable, although on sharp curves the couplers sometimes separate by themselves.

Lionel's design functioned electrically, although the style, activating method or means of current pickup changed almost yearly until the war. The coupler itself was a cast box, pivoted at the back and with a lip at the front that descended over and held the hook on an adjacent coupler. This design allowed Lionel owners to couple the newer cars with older latch coupler-equipped cars. Because the company mounted them at different heights, however, cars from the 1938-1942 era do not all couple together with ease. Flyer's coupler changes are also a real problem for operators with equipment made in different years; they went from hooks through harpoons to sheet metal knuckles (usually called curly-Q) to latches, and most are incompatible.

The first automatic design from Lionel had an electromagnet that attracted a plate on the coupler box, causing it to pivot upward and release the next car's hook. Current was supplied through a metal shoe underneath the truck that received power from a special ramp described below. The circuit grounded through the car's wheels.

The main flaw in this design was the exposed metal pickup shoe. When a car passed over a switch, the shoe would momentarily touch the third rail, powering the electromagnet, and cars would frequently release unexpectedly. To address this problem, Lionel introduced a design with Bakelite (plastic) shoes surrounding the metal contacts. These shoes had raised shoulders that guided the contacts along the uncoupling ramp rails, but raised them above the third rails of switches. The concept worked, although the shape of the shoe on early cars sometimes causes them

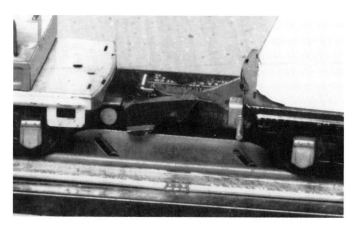

When pushed up by the mechanical action of the uncoupling ramp blades, the notches on American Flyer couplers rise to release the pins, and allow the cars to separate.

The first automatic box coupler from Lionel was opened by magnetic attraction, and the exposed pickup shoe could be triggered by the third rail on a switch, causing unexpected separations.

Lionel finally succeeded in producing a reliable automatic coupler, with a protected pickup shoe and solenoid-activated release mechanism, but it was short-lived. The new knuckle coupler was introduced in 1945.

to catch on various kinds of trackwork, usually resulting in a broken shoe.

The actuating mechanism was also changed, to a solenoid design that pushed a control rod against the plate attached to the back of the box. These couplers worked reasonably well, and by 1942 Lionel had perfected the box coupler, only to replace it with a superior knuckle design after the war, making Pre- and Postwar equipment incompatible.

To operate these couplers, a special five-rail ramp was introduced, attached to which (by a four-wire cable) was a double button box labeled "uncouple" and "unload." The two extra rails were placed equidistant from each of the running rails and the center power rail. When a car passed over the ramp, the pickup shoes contacted these rails, which normally had no power flowing through them.

When the operator pushed the "uncouple" button on the box, power was fed to both of these inner rails, and thus to the uncoupler shoe, which triggered the activating magnet or solenoid, causing the coupler to open. The circuit grounded through the car's wheels.

This simple device also operated Lionel's attractive and interesting automatic cars of the late '30s and early '40s. These cars variously dumped coal, logs or barrels, or tossed packing crates out of boxcar doors.

When the "unload" button was pressed on the control box, a different set of contacts was engaged through a series of flexible metal leaves. In this mode, one of the ramp rails received power, while the other was grounded. This triggered the solenoid that dumped the freight,

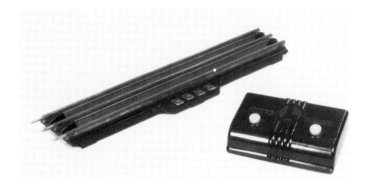

This five-rail ramp supplied current to the shoes on Lionel cars, activating the couplers or action devices that dumped coal, logs, barrels and packing crates.

and also operated the coupler on one end (the one whose shoe was resting on the control rail that received the power; the grounded shoe did not react). This was not a problem, as the train was normally stopped in neutral during dumping operations, and the coupler box would drop down again before the train was restarted.

These uncoupling ramps are readily available in both O and O27 configurations; the O27 type mates easily with Gargraves trackage. However, I do not use them, as I am not always exactly sure where I will need them when I am laying my flexible track, and it is inconvenient to remove track at a later date to insert these ramps. Nor do I like their appearance. Fortunately, it is both easy and inexpensive to custom build a substitute, and install it any time and at any place on the layout without disturbing existing installations. These homemade uncouplers can even be placed on curves, whereas Lionel's units are all straight.

All that is needed can be obtained from an electrical supply store or hobby shop: a coil of ¼-inch aluminum ground cable, a normally "open" push button and a center-off DPDT (double-pole, double-throw) toggle switch. Two foot-long pieces of ground cable are formed into control rails, with an inch bent down at right angles at each end. These are inserted into holes drilled between the ties, so that they are equidistant from the running and power rails, just like Lionel's ramps.

Lengths of aluminum ground cable can be inserted between the rails at any point on the layout, to serve as contact rails for the pickup shoes on Lionel's automatic cars.

If the holes drilled in the layout are exactly ¼ inch, the ground cable will stay at the right height, held in place by the friction of the wooden table top. These rails should be aligned just slightly below the level of the center rail, to avoid contact with lighted car and whistle tender rollers.

Wiring these ramps is simple, as shown in the diagram, and provides a constant fixed voltage which allows operating cars to function even when no power is applied to the track. (Lionel ramps need track power to work unless specially wired, so locomotives must stand in neutral during these maneuvers.) Tracing these wires will show that with the DPDT switch in the down position, 14 volts is routed to both control rails when the push button is pressed. With the switch up, one rail receives this power, while the other is grounded. "Up" unloads, and "down" uncouples, at the touch of a button.

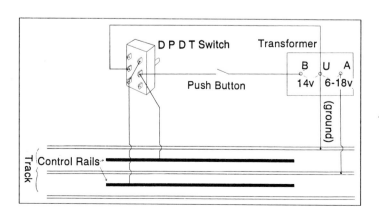

The pattern of wiring a double-pole, double-throw switch to the uncoupling ramp control rails allows 14 volts to be fed to each rail when the switch is in the down position, and to only one rail when the switch is up. In the up position, the other rail is grounded. Pushing the button closes the circuit.

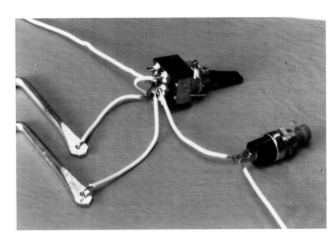

When wired, the do-it-yourself control parts look like this. All that can be seen from the front of the operator's panel are the toggle switch and the push button.

One caution is in order: a center-off DPDT toggle switch should be used. Some toggles have only two positions (in this case, "up" and "down"), and would ground one rail when left in the up position. Alternatively, the switch may always be left in the uncouple (down) position, but a center-off switch tells the operator when the rails are electrically neutral, without ambiguity. A grounded control rail invites the possibility of short circuits caused by pickup rollers.

Soldering wires to the aluminum ground cable is difficult, and is not really desirable, as it makes removing the control rails at a later date more difficult. Instead I flatten one end with a hammer and file it to the proper size for insertion into the table, then drill a tiny hole to receive the feed wire, which is wrapped tightly around the aluminum after connection. Several wraps will ensure positive and permanent contact.

The control boxes on Lionel's ramps are bulky, and take up a lot of room on a control panel. They are also prone to trouble, as the various copper contacts inside often oxidize and impede current flow, or lose their alignment and fail to make the proper sequence of electrical connections. Modelers who wish to use these ramps may also apply the push button and DPDT switch approach, as shown in the diagram of a Lionel RCS ramp.

Having examined the types of track and related accessories available, it is time to discuss how these can be wired for maximum control and efficiency. In this context we will explore the process of putting down the track and getting the action started.

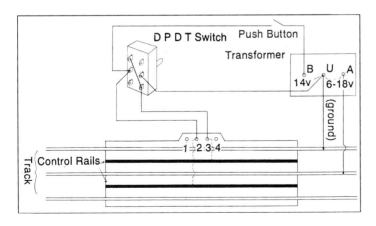

Using this wiring method, Lionel's own uncoupling ramps may receive fixed voltage power without the inconvenience of the bulky control boxes. This also eliminates two of the four wires leading to the ramp, a decided advantage for distant locations. This diagram is appropriate for all RCS and 1019 ramps, Prewar and Postwar, and for the Postwar 6019. To adapt it to the Postwar UCS model, the wire connected to post 2 should be attached to post 1 instead.

SIX

Wiring Made Easy

In order to perform well, toy trains need a consistent supply of reliable electrical power, delivered without interruption to motors, lights and accessories. Additionally, the engineer must have sufficient control over the distribution of this power to ensure the right amount reaching the right places at the right times. The system must be safe, efficient and relatively easy to maintain, and should be designed to allow for changes and additions without major renovation. It must have adequate capacity for the size of the layout being built, but should not be unduly expensive. And if we are to remain faithful to our toy heritage, it should reflect a technology consistent with the trains themselves.

This may sound complicated, but all of these qualities are within grasp, with the possible exception of economy. The basis for the power distribution system (and its most expensive element) is the power source itself, the toy train transformer.

During the earliest years of this century, few homes outside of major urban areas were equipped with electricity. The first train sets were designed to operate on power from batteries, usually of the dry cell variety, which were not cheap.

For homes that had power installed, Lionel provided instructions for attaching a lamp socket to acid-based wet cells, which in turn were connected to the train track. It was probably cheaper than buying dry cells which could not be recharged, but the danger inherent in allowing children to play with such chemicals is frightening to consider.

To complicate matters, electrical power was not standardized throughout the continent. Some areas had direct current (DC), with voltage set at either 110 or 220. Alternating current (AC) was the norm elsewhere, but the frequency of alternation was not uniform, being 25, 50 or 60 cycles, depending on the generating equipment used.

With the advent of his Standard Gauge line in 1906, Joshua Lionel Cowen began producing current reducers for homes with electrical service. These came in three configurations: two for AC of 110 and 220 volts, and one for DC at 110 volts. Eventually (1914) a 220-volt DC reducer was also produced. While still not entirely safe, these were a great improvement over wet cells, and much more economical than the disposable dry cells. Nevertheless, a more versatile method of providing low voltage was needed.

A transformer is a relatively simple device that functions by a principle known as induction. House current is passed through a coil of wire (the primary coil) having a predetermined number of turns; this induces a magnetic field. The field generates a similar current in an adjacent coil made up of a greater number of turns of thinner wire. The resultant voltage reduction is a function of the relationship between the size and number of turns in the two fields. The finer wire, called the secondary coil, generates voltage low enough to be suitable for small toy train motors.

Lionel introduced its first transformers in 1914. They were housed in cast-iron cases and had a handle attached to a primitive metal contact lever which could be moved from one to another of a series of metal studs, which were connected to various points on the secondary coil. Depending upon the number of turns of the coil between each stud and the end of the field, varying amounts of voltage were directed to the track when the handle was advanced.

This design was steadily refined, and was eventually encased in sheet metal beginning in 1922; it continued in production through 1938. The only drawback was a momentary interruption in power as the control handle passed from stud to stud. The voltage normally increased between studs in increments or "steps" of two volts, which led to the nickname "step transformer" for these units.

This design caused no serious problems until the introduction of automatic reversing units, which were triggered by a break in the current. For trains equipped with this device, which Lionel called "Distant Control," a rheostat was supplied which was spliced into one of the feed wires to the track. This consisted of a coil of resistance wire over which a contact rubbed, passing varying amounts of current depending upon where this coil was tapped by the contact. Rheostats allowed the smooth, stepless increase or decrease of voltage without interruption.

To provide uninterrupted power and variable voltage to the track when using batteries or a step-type transformer, rheostats such as these (numbers 81 and 88) were wired into the circuit.

Other manufacturers such as American Flyer began combining the rheostat and transformer in a single housing in the early 1930s, but Lionel did not do so until later in the decade. They were not of a complicated design; the rheostat dial simply wiped a contact arm over the secondary coil, giving it an infinite number of taps instead of the handful provided by the studs, with no breaks in the power flow.

Purchasers could obtain toy transformers without buying complete trains sets, and one supplier, the Jefferson Manufacturing Company, produced a large number of units which can still be found today, often in working condition. Like those built by American Flyer, they incorporated a rheostat well before Lionel, and in fact were sometimes included in Lionel sets.

Lionel's transformers were safe and reliable, and came in a number of sizes with different power ratings. The smallest (labeled "A" by the company) produced 40 watts of power, suitable

American Flyer and Jefferson made transformers with case-mounted dial rheostats beginning in the early 1930s. These units eliminated the external speed control that was necessary for Lionel transformers when operating locomotives with automatic reversing.

Lionel's small A and B Multivolt Transformers produced 40 and 75 watts respectively, while the much larger model K generated 150. Note the screw-type electrical connector on the line cord of the model B, the oldest unit in this group (c. 1919). Many homes which had electric lights at that time still had no wall receptacles, and appliances had to be connected through lamp sockets. The wall plug on the later model A transformer still has the protective wooden box in which it was packed.

only for O Gauge motors. Those designated B, C, T and K produced up to 200 watts, and were suitable for Standard Gauge trains; the largest could also run a considerable number of accessories and lamps. They could be tapped for a wide range of fixed and variable voltages, and were called "Multivolt Transformers" in Lionel advertising.

In different locations on the North American continent, homes were supplied with alternating current which oscillated at rates other than the common 60 cycles per second. (60-cycle current is nearly universal now in the United States and Canada. This contributes to the absolute accuracy of electric clocks, which are easily geared to this frequency because of their 60-seconds-to-the-minute, 60-minutes-to-the-hour relationships.) At one time both 25-cycle and 50-cycle current could be found; the former was common in Nova Scotia, where I now make my home.

Transformers built for 60-cycle current would overheat when operated on lower frequencies, and therefore Lionel produced alternate units for markets such as Atlantic Canada. The Prewar transformers most often found in Nova Scotia are Lionel's WX 25-cycle models. I frequently use them; they operate satisfactorily on today's 60-cycle power, although they produce lower voltages.

Lionel began incorporating rheostats in small-sized transformers in the latter 1930s, culminating in a series of superior designs which came in four sizes: 50-watt (model Q), 100-watt (R), 150-watt (V) and 250-watt (Z). The two largest had four separate rheostats controlling four variable circuits; the model R had two. They could be wired to control multiple numbers of trains, or used to power accessories and light lamps.

Largest of all Prewar transformers, Lionel's powerful model Z produced 250 watts and could operate as many as four separate trains, or a large number of lamps and accessories.

These transformers had no provision for breaking the current to activate the locomotive's reversing E-unit, other than twisting the dial to the "off" position. Nor was a whistle control included. A separate control box containing a normally "on" push button and a rectifier that produced about a volt and a half of DC current could be purchased and spliced into the track feed wire. The former device interrupted the power for reversing, and the latter activated the DC relay on the whistle motor.

These new models received the trademark "Trainmaster," and were continued briefly after the war, soon to be replaced by similar but improved units with

Beginning in 1938, some Lionel sets included transformers with built-in whistle controllers, such as this 1040 model.

built-in reversing and whistle controls. These are described later in this chapter.

The Trainmaster transformers were relatively expensive, and Lionel included lower priced models with less output in prepackaged train sets. Some of these incorporated rectifiers for the whistle, such as No. 1040 of 1938 and 1939. (This one came with my sister's 1939 set, which I inherited when her interest shifted to other things.)

Meanwhile, American Flyer was producing a competing line of power transformers of various ratings, and like Lionel's, they have proven to be very durable. A transformer is a relatively simple device, and will last for decades if not abused. Countless Zs and Vs continue in use today; the only maintenance they usually need is occasional replacement of the carbon rollers that make contact with the secondary coil to provide variable voltage. Sometimes the plugs and line cords deteriorate, and must also be replaced. Most of the old step-types still work, too. Since they perform so well, can there be any reasons not to use them for our period layouts? Unfortunately, the answer may be yes.

Antique Power: Pros and Cons

The strongest argument for using original Prewar transformers is the authenticity of their appearance, and whenever I assemble a show layout (such as the one that circles an on-stage tree at my annual Acadia University Christmas Concert) I use one. The older types without rheostats are simply not practical for any kind of operation that requires fine speed control, however. The two-volt jumps between steps prevent smooth acceleration, and the momentary breaks in current activate a locomotive's reverse unit. For non-reversing trains running on a loop, they can be fine, but lack the sophistication needed for anything more complex.

Standard Gauge operators often use them because their high voltage output (up to 25 volts) is needed for the large motors in these toys. Whereas Standard Gauge was declining during the 1930s and never enjoyed such enhancements as automatic uncoupling, more refined control is not as critical, and a rheostat can always be wired into the circuit (although the original Lionel units often overheat and suffer considerable voltage drop).

Step transformers can be used, however, to provide a source of fixed voltage for lamps and accessories, especially if the transformers used to run the trains are not large enough for this

Prior to the introduction of transformers with built-in whistle controllers, a separate unit such as Lionel's No. 66 or 167 was spliced into the track wiring. These devices lowered the operating voltage that reached the locomotive by about five volts.

added burden. Many modelers follow this approach, although I do not for reasons of wiring economy, as discussed below under the topic of common ground.

Rheostat-equipped units, and especially those in the Trainmaster series, are much more practical. They do require a whistle control box, however, and this device has one irritating flaw: it lowers the track voltage by about five volts, and there are a few Prewar O Gauge locos that need the extra power, as do most Lionel Standard Gauge locomotives. There is a way around it: a simple whistle blower can be made from a dry cell and a single-pole, double-throw toggle switch.

The hot lead from the transformer is wired to the center terminal of the SPDT switch. Each of the outer terminals is connected to the third rail of the track, one directly and one through the dry cell. When the switch is thrown so that the current passes to the train through the battery instead of directly from the transformer, the tender-mounted whistle will blow.

A size D dry cell wired as shown will blow Lionel's tender-mounted whistles, which operate by a DC relay. A battery box of the type available from Radio Shack may be used for convenience. The SPDT switch should not have a center-off position, and should be thrown as quickly as possible to prevent tripping the locomotive's reverse unit.

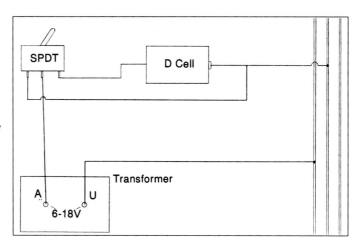

At this point I am forced to admit to another minor deviation from my adherence to Prewar practice. In other words, I cheat!

Beginning in the late 1940s, Lionel produced two magnificent transformers, made in huge quantities and still readily available (although recent prices are approaching the height of the ozone layer!). The mighty ZW (in either 250-watt or the later 275-watt form) contains four variable circuits, two of which are equipped with reversing and whistle controls. It can deliver a full 21 volts of power at the terminals. Almost as versatile is the KW, a 190-watt model with two variable circuits for running, reversing and whistling two trains, and several different fixed voltage circuits. These transformers have great capacity for even the largest layouts, and my current layout uses two of each.

Engineers with lesser requirements might investigate two other models: the RW at 110 watts, and the extremely durable and dependable 90-watt No. 1033. Both are single-train units with whistle and reverse controls and numerous fixed voltage combinations for accessories. They

The finest toy train transformers for Prewar or Postwar use are Lionel's versatile 275-watt ZW and 190-watt KW models. The former can operate up to four trains at once. Either one can run two trains and still provide for multiple operating accessories.

operate smoothly and were made in very large quantities. Unfortunately, safety regulations in the United States currently restrict the manufacture of large capacity transformers designed for use by children, and more and more modelers are chasing fewer and fewer of these older units, so the prices keep rising. (The reason for these regulations escapes me; I have never heard of any serious mishap with a Lionel transformer, but that may be my ignorance. Recently, however, a 400-watt model was introduced by Right-Of-Way Industries, although the price is very high.)

Other models are available, including Lionel LW, TW and 1044 models, and a whole range of American Flyer Postwar products that generate up to 300 watts of power. These Flyer transformers peak at about 17 volts output, however, and Prewar trains, especially when combined with lots of accessories, often need more.

This rollaway platform allows the transformers to be stored under the table when not in use, conserving valuable aisle area.

Any fairly large layout will usually require more than one transformer, and I have experimented with a number of locations for these bulky items in relation to the control panel. Wherever they are placed, they either steal valuable table space (and also detract visually) from the trains or intrude upon aisle space.

The latter condition is not a problem during operation, but can be a real nuisance when one is working on the layout. To overcome this drawback, I designed a rollaway power center, mounted on casters and extending just 28 inches above the floor, with the transformers mounted on top. This is a comfortable height for manipulating the controls, and is just low enough to allow the entire unit to roll under the layout when not in use, completely out of the way during building or maintenance chores.

The transformers are connected by flexible wires to terminal strips under the layout, from which all other wiring extends. This simple system also allows for the easiest possible substitution of replacement transformers whenever repairs are needed.

Admittedly these power units look very modern in a Prewar setting, but are not really considered to be a visual part of the layout. Unless a totally integrated period appearance is desired, I recommend the use of the extremely versatile Postwar transformers instead of the early designs.

Now we have to get the current to the track.

A Common Ground

Although the concept is simple and familiar to anyone versed in the basics of electricity, the advantages of a common ground wire are sometimes overlooked. The theory is simple; every circuit must have two wires, one to provide the power to the motor, lamp or coil, and one to return it to the source. This is in fact how direct current (DC) flows, in a steady stream from one battery terminal to the other. While alternating current (AC) changes direction sixty times per second, it is still helpful to conceive of it as flowing from the hot (power) wire to the ground terminal.

One terminal on the transformer is designated the ground. While in terms of AC electric flow it doesn't matter which terminal this is, in practical terms most transformers are designed so that one terminal serves a variety of functions when combined with the other posts. It forms a ground for all the circuits controlled by the various rheostats, and provides fixed voltages in conjunction with other terminals. This ground post is usually (but not always) labeled "U" on Lionel Postwar transformers.

When setting up the initial wiring for a layout, I first run a ground wire from one of the U terminals to all those areas where track and accessories will be located, then back to another U post. This usually takes the form of a large circle of wire beneath the table which is shaped approximately the same as the loop of track it will serve. (I use a very heavy 12- or 14-gauge wire for the ground. This is excessively thick, but ensures against voltage drop over long distances.)

Each section of track and every accessory can now be connected to the ground wire at the nearest possible meeting point, using a minimum of wire. From this point on, powering each item requires only one wire from the transformer, the so-called hot wire. I have seen layouts where every siding, main line and operating accessory received a pair of wires directly from the transformer, when only one would have been needed with the common ground system. This is just simple common sense, but is not always readily apparent to the inexperienced.

Having elected to adopt the common ground approach, it now becomes important for the builder to wire the track in such a manner that the ground wire can always be located easily. To aid visually in this, I use black wire for the ground. All other colors of wires are chosen according to the function they perform.

Each track section now receives three feeder wires; remember that I am using flexible track in which all three rails (two for the wheels and the center one for power) are insulated from each other. I designate the outside rail (the one always toward the edge of the table) as the ground, and attach to it a short black feeder wire. The center rail (power) receives a red feeder, and the inner rail (on the side opposite the edge of the table) a green feeder. Color photo 6 shows these wires in place.

The flexible track sections should first be curved and trimmed to fit in their eventual locations on the layout, as the bending process causes the individual rails to slide in the grooves of the wooden ties. They should be carefully test fit until the exact desired shape is achieved.

Attaching the wires to the track is easy, as each rail is hollow and slotted on the bottom. I bend the end of each wire in a small loop and hammer it flat, then slide two adjacent ties away from each other to expose a longer segment of the underside of the rail, and insert the flattened wire into the slot in the rail. Then I slide the ties back toward each other, thus compressing the sides of the rail to hold the wire snugly. This procedure is shown in the two photographs of the underside of a section of track. (Although some modelers solder the wire to the track, I have never found it necessary; it is both time consuming and more difficult to undo, should changes in the track plan be undertaken.)

The track may now be placed in its proper location on the layout. The spots where the feed wires protrude are marked on the table top, and a small hole is drilled for each. The three wires are inserted in the holes, and the track section is lowered into place. If the locations for the holes are accurate, the wires are now virtually invisible.

The end of the track section should have two brass connector pins, one in the outside ground rail and one in the center power rail. The inside running rail (hereafter called the *control* rail) has an insulating fiber or plastic pin instead of a brass one. This pin may be omitted entirely and the rail ends left empty, but I prefer to insert one to assure that this rail stays in correct alignment, and to prevent it from touching the rail on the next section of track, should any shifting take place due to expansion or vibration. These insulating pins are available commercially, or may be made of scrap plastic strips of the proper size to slip into the rail ends.

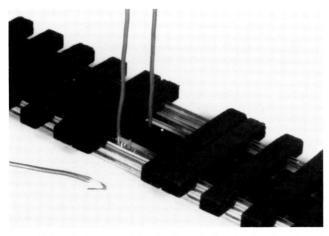 

A small loop is hammered flat in the end of each wire, then inserted into the slot in the bottom of the rail between two ties. When the ties are slid toward each other, friction keeps the wire in place and provides good electrical contact.

I use Lionel O27 insulating pins for this purpose. They are cheap and readily available, and have a short center section of increased diameter that keeps the rail ends apart. They are too thick for the flexible rails, however, and must be trimmed to fit with a modeling knife. Insulating pins designed to fit Gargraves rails are also available from some suppliers.

For utmost versatility, every track section should have its control rail insulated at both ends. This allows for the maximum number of possibilities for triggering accessory mechanisms, as described below. Especially important is an insulator wherever the track is attached to a Lionel track switch, as their running rails are grounded together.

Track laying continues until the entire loop is completed. If the whole line is to be powered at all times by the same rheostat, then the center (power) rail is continuous, with brass pins connecting all of the sections together. If some of the sections are to be operated by a different rheostat, or controlled by a device such as an automatic-stop station, plastic connectors are used in the third rail to isolate these sections electrically. Every track section should now have three wires extending below the table top.

The first step is to connect all of the black feeder wires to the previously installed black ground wire at the nearest possible locations. This provides a highly reliable ground, as it is connected to the transformer at both ends of the heavy black loop, and is also continuous through the brass rail joiners. (Critics may accuse me of overkill, but having spent many hours trouble-shooting layouts with faulty grounds, I prefer too many connections to too few.)

The feeder wires from the track may be soldered to the wires below the table, but this is an awkward job which can result in drops of hot solder dripping on the floor, carpet or one's clothing. It is also harder to dismantle later.

I prefer a mechanical connection. Small solderless lugs (available from hobby shops) are crimped on the ends of the feed wires. An electrician's wire stripper is used to expose a short

Wires from above the table can be connected without the use of solder by crimping a lug on the end and screwing it into the underside of the table over the wire to which it is to be fastened.

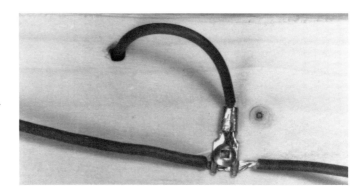

length of the ground wire, and the lug is then placed over it and screwed to the table with a ⅜" x #4 screw. This screw is too short to penetrate the upper surface of the table, but is sufficient to make secure contact.

The second step is to connect a power wire to a variable voltage post of the transformer. This wire should also be of heavy gauge to prevent voltage drop at distant points. If desired (and I highly recommend this), such a power wire should be run through an on-off toggle switch located on the control panel, to allow the engineer to cut off power to that portion of the track. If the entire loop is to operate from one rheostat, only one such wire is needed, and it is located under the table in the same approximate pattern as the track above it. All of the red feeder wires are then attached to it.

If the loop is divided into two or more electrically independent "blocks" or lengths of track (such as to provide for control by two rheostats), two power wires are required, one from the A post to one block, the other from the B post to the second block. The diagram shows such an arrangement, which allows for independent control of two trains as long as each one occupies a different block, or allows differing amounts of current to be applied to each. This is advantageous under certain circumstances. For example, a block on an upgrade could receive extra voltage to aid in hill-climbing, while the downgrade receives less voltage to retard the descending speed of the locomotive, without the engineer having to adjust the speed control when the train reaches the top of the grade.

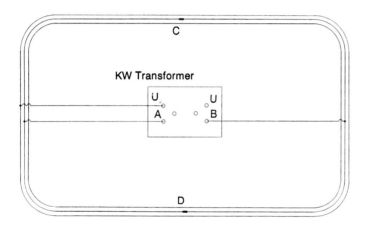

The track loop is divided into two electrically independent halves by fiber or plastic insulating pins in the center rails at points C and D. The power wire from rheostat A is attached to one half of the loop, and that from the other rheostat (post B) is attached to the other half. The ground post (U) serves both circuits. The speed of a train in one half of the loop can now be controlled independently of one in the other half.

Wiring In Accessories

We now have an operating loop of track, with all ground and power wires connected to the transformer. The green wires from the control rails are still unused, however, but they provide almost unlimited flexibility in the addition of accessories at any point on the layout.

Let us assume that a Lionel No. 45 crossing gateman is to be added, but the modeler has not planned in advance the exact location of the highway it is meant to protect, or decides to change it from the original plan. The control rails allow the gateman to be placed anywhere! The modeler chooses the site, drills two holes for its wires, and screws the base of the accessory to the table. Next, a wire is connected between a fixed 14-volt transformer post and one of the gateman's wires through a toggle switch, which allows the unit to be turned off if desired.

Making the gateman operate is now a cinch. Every 3-foot section of track, with its insulated control rail, is a potential activator. One chooses the spot where the locomotive will be when the gateman should emerge from his shed, then identifies the green control wire attached to that section. This is attached to the other wire of the accessory.

The gateman is now connected to 14 volts of ungrounded power, so the circuit is not complete. However, when a locomotive or car enters the section of track containing the attached control rail, the wheels bridge the gap between it and the ground rail. The circuit is now completed and power flows through, causing the gateman to come out waving his lantern.

This method allows for the addition of gates, bells, lights or whistle stations at any point where a control rail can be found (which on my layout is everywhere!), and allows for easy relocation whenever one is in the mood for a change. It can also be used to trip a relay, preventing collisions between two trains on the same loop of track and changing block signals from green to red. These tricks are described later in this chapter.

On a layout using regular sectional toy train track, special sections containing control rails must be made by the modeler. One of the running

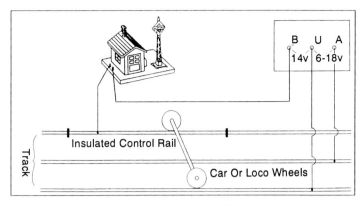

Using the control rail method for the automatic operation of an accessory, 14 volts of current is routed to one of its wires, while the other is connected to the control rail. When the wheels of a loco or car enter the track section, a ground is completed through them, and the accessory operates. This No. 45 gateman, one of Lionel's earliest animated accessories, comes out of his shed swinging a red plastic lantern illuminated from below by a bulb in the base. A photo appears in Chapter Nine.

rails is removed by prying up the metal tabs that hold it to the ties. Fiber insulators are then placed between the rail and each tie, before the rail is put back in place. Electrical tape may be used as an insulating material if fiber spacers (such as the ones factory installed on the center rail) are not available.

Fiber or plastic rail-joining pins are used to insulate both ends of the control rail, and a wire is led from it to the accessory which is to be activated. This is a fussy job, but running accessories in this way is still more reliable than using the pressure-activated contactors of the immediate Prewar and entire Postwar periods.

Transformers

The layout described in this book has four independent loops of track, or main lines. The switches making up the crossover tracks between them are fully insulated from each other with plastic rail joiners in all three rails. A separate transformer powers each loop, KWs on the outer and the elevated ones, and a ZW on each of the other two. These transformers are plugged into the house wiring so that they are "in phase," which allows trains to pass from one loop to another (and thus from the control of one transformer to another) without causing a short circuit.

Phasing two transformers is easy. A wire is connected from the ground (U) post of one to the ground post of the other, and both units are plugged in and their rheostats set so that about twelve volts of current is being produced by each. Then a wire is connected to the hot (rheostat-controlled) post of one transformer, and touched lightly to the hot post of the other. If a heavy spark occurs, the wall plug on one transformer is removed from the wall and rotated 180 degrees. The transformers are now safely in phase. (I mark all the plugs on my transformers to indicate which way they should be plugged in, saving me the trouble of rephasing them every time one is removed and replaced.)

I use the massive 275-watt ZW transformers for powering two or more segments of a loop with the two rheostats that contain direction and whistle controls. The other two rheostats are set to provide fixed voltages: usually one at 14 volts for operating accessories, and one at 10 to 12 volts for lamps. The ZW has plenty of reserve power to handle the trains and a large number of lamps. Operating accessories are less of a drain on the total power available, as they are usually used only when the train is standing still and consuming no voltage.

The KW units are installed the same way, although I use them less for accessories for two reasons. Their lower rating (190 watts) means less power going to the trains. Furthermore, the most often-used fixed voltage circuit, 14 volts, is not provided through the common ground posts

(U), but by posts C and D. This requires two wires from the transformer to any accessory, rather than one.

The fixed voltages available with a common ground may be used for lamps, however. The life span of a miniature light bulb is greatly increased if it is operated on voltage lower than its optimum rating. A 14-volt bulb does not burn as brightly on 10 volts, but actually looks more realistic and lasts much, much longer. The KW's D post provides 20 volts when grounded. Therefore two bulbs wired in series will receive 10 volts each from this post, and may be wired to the common ground, saving the running of a second wire from the transformer, as shown in the accompanying diagram.

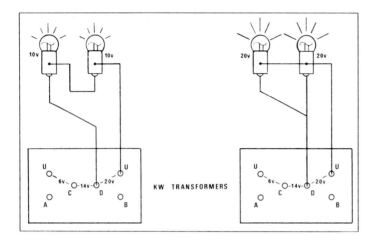

The diagram on the left shows two 14-volt bulbs wired in series to a 20-volt fixed voltage post and the common ground. This method provides 10 volts to each bulb, and extends their life span considerably. The other diagram illustrates parallel wiring, in which 20 volts would be fed to each of the 14-volt bulbs (giving them roughly the same life expectancy as a pork chop in a lion's cage!).

It should now be apparent why I do not use an auxiliary transformer to power lamps and accessories. The advantages of the common ground system are simply too great to ignore (especially the savings in wire!), and these big Lionel Postwar power plants can handle the job by themselves.

It is possible to connect the ground posts of all transformers together, but I do not recommend this, and prefer to keep them all independent. The only time two transformers are connected on my layout is during the brief period when a train is passing from one loop to the other. When a layout is wired in this manner, troubleshooting is much easier. Short circuits are more localized and simpler to find, and spreading the load equally among each of the transformers is more easily accomplished. My layout has four separate ground wire loops, one for each transformer, and tracing the circuits when repairs or modifications are required is an easy task.

The average model railroad looks like the interior of a Bell Telephone Company relay station when viewed from the underside; wires go everywhere! Bringing order out of this chaos, and allowing the engineer full mastery over all operations, is the function of a well-designed and intelligently conceived control panel. The following tricks allow the creation of a neat, professional-looking panel that is not only easy to use or to change, but requires virtually no drilling for the installation of switches and indicator lights.

The Control Panel

I like to run trains! I also enjoy the time spent in building layouts, but some tasks are repetitive and unrewarding, so I consider the elimination of such jobs to be its own reward, in terms of time saved for running the trains some more.

In all my years as a modeler, I must have drilled thousands of quarter-inch holes in control panels for the insertion of miniature toggle switches. It's no fun! Not only is it boring, but despite advance planning of the caliber of Solomon's wisdom, some of those holes will end up in the wrong place when the panel is completed. Empty holes annoy me, and I used to leave an unused toggle switch in place, so visitors never knew of my mistake. But I knew!

I have now discovered a method of building control panels without ever drilling another hole! Furthermore, the panel can be changed, the toggles relocated, and the wiring rerouted without ever facing an empty hole or unconnected switch again.

The face of the panel is made from a sheet of pegboard perforated with ¼-inch holes, available from any building supply firm. Electronic supply shops market a wide range of miniature toggle switches and push buttons with ¼-inch shanks that fit snugly and securely in these holes. However, a panel full of unused holes is not too attractive, so before any switches are installed, we need a smooth, unblemished surface.

The solution comes from the housewares section of any hardware or department store, in the form of adhesive-backed vinyl shelf covering, which is available in a variety of shades. I have used solid colors and a dark wood-grained pattern on previous panels, but the white covering shown in the accompanying photograph has proven to be the most attractive and easy on the eyes. This material has a tough surface, but can be cut easily wherever necessary.

The adhesive does not always stick well to the pegboard's surface, but a little contact cement around the edges provides a more permanent bond. The result is a solid-looking panel that is ready to accept toggle switches in any location, while your power drill gathers dust in the corner.

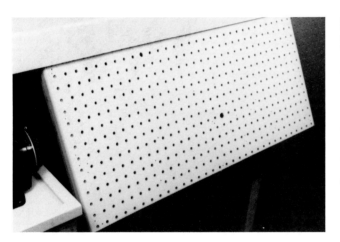 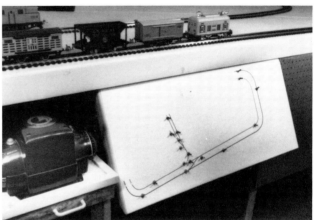

A sheet of pegboard with ¼-inch holes provides an ideal pre-drilled control panel. Covering the surface with adhesive vinyl provides an attractive appearance, and hides those holes where switches will not be installed.

The panel is now ready for the addition of the track plan. This can be laid out on the surface using flexible tape from an artist's supply house; it comes in a wide variety of colors. The product I use is 1⁄16-inch-wide "Letraline" made by the Letraset Corporation. Each of my four main lines is represented by a different color. Sidings appear in the same color as the main line to which they connect, to allow for quick identification of the correct transformer to use when running trains there.

Gaps in the tape represent points in the track plan where insulated rail joiners are installed in the third rail. This permits easy identification of blocks, and allows the operator to tell at a glance which throttle to use for any given section of track. The track plan need not be accurate in scale, but should approximate closely the actual design of the track, as this aids the engineer in identifying which switches to throw for each desired function.

The toggle switches I use come with removable plastic covers for the handles, in green, red, yellow and white. I use a different color for each function: red for track blocks, green for relays, yellow for lamps and white for accessories. A different style with a black handle is used for uncouple/unload ramps.

Normally "open" push buttons were used on my previous layout to operate the No. 1121 track switches (which from this point on I will refer to as *turnouts* to avoid confusion with the toggles). These come in red only, and serve in this natural state to identify the buttons that set turnouts to the *curve* position. Push buttons for *straight* are painted green. An alternative method sacrifices the visual advantage of the two color-coded push buttons, but requires only

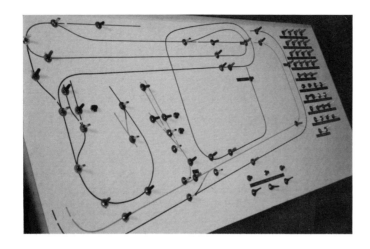

Flexible tape is ideal for creating a representation of the track plan on the surface of the control panel. Switches may be located wherever needed by cutting out a circle of vinyl above any of the holes in the pegboard. Labels made with a vinyl label maker are placed wherever needed, such as to identify the function of a toggle switch.

one device: a single-pole, double-throw switch with spring return to center-off position. I employed this method on the current layout, as described later in the chapter.

Installing these switches and buttons is very simple. Once the desired location is decided upon, a modeler's knife is used to cut out the circle of vinyl over the nearest available pegboard hole. The switch is inserted, its securing collar screwed on, and the job is complete, giving a neat appearance in record time with no drilling, sawdust or frustration. Wires may now be attached to the terminals of the switch behind the panel, and connected to the transformer and layout as needed.

Should a switch ever need ever need to be repositioned, thus leaving an empty hole, it is an easy matter to cover it with a piece of vinyl. Major reorganizations of the panel are best accomplished by starting over with a fresh vinyl covering over the entire surface. This takes a surprisingly small amount of time, a fraction of that required to install a new solid panel surface and drill all the holes that are needed.

Some of the switches should be marked for identification, especially those that turn lights and accessories off and on. A vinyl label maker is ideal for this purpose. These labels stick well to the surface, yet can be peeled off if necessary. They are easy to read and take up very little space.

The size of the control panel is a matter of personal choice. It should be large enough to permit the installation of all necessary switches without crowding, but should detract as little as possible from space in the room. Mine is 32 inches wide by 14 inches high, and is mounted at an angle as shown in the photographs. It is located beside the transformer table, which is convenient during operation and close enough for economical wiring practices. It would have to be much larger, however, if I were to use Lionel's bulky turnout and uncoupling ramp controllers. Fortunately, these are easily replaced by tiny devices that can be located in the appropriate places on the track diagram.

Chapter Five describes the toggle and push button method of operating the uncouple/unload ramps. Each installation requires only two holes in the pegboard. In a similar manner, two push buttons or an SPDT toggle can be used to control any Lionel turnout, or the switch machine that moves a Gargraves or Right-Of-Way turnout.

Examination of any Lionel turnout will reveal three terminal screws, to which three wires leading from a control box are attached. The principle behind their operation is very simple. One of these terminals (the center one on a 1121 turnout) is a ground. The other two are connected to opposite ends of a solenoid which moves the turnout rails. All the control box does (besides lighting a red or green lamp) is complete the circuit between the center ground terminal and one of the solenoid wires. Depending upon which way the control lever is moved, it causes the solenoid to push the rails to either the curved or straight position. Because the voltage to operate the turnout comes from the third rail, there must be power in the track for them to operate. (Lionel's O Gauge 022 turnouts have a provision for a fixed voltage plug, and are therefore independent of track power.)

Lionel's turnout control box takes up a huge amount of space on the panel. Two normally "open" push buttons will serve the same purpose. One push button is connected between the ground and each of the two outer terminal posts on the turnout. Pushing either of the buttons grounds the solenoid and throws the turnout rails. These buttons are located on the control panel near to the turnout location on the track diagram.

Alternatively, an SPDT (single-pole, double throw) toggle switch with a spring return to a center-off position may be substituted for the two push buttons. The ground is connected to the center post on this toggle, and the two control wires from the turnout are soldered to the other two. Moving the toggle up or down throws the turnout, and the spring return automatically disconnects the ground when the toggle is released. A DPDT (double-pole, double-throw) toggle switch of the same design may be used to light simultaneously a red bulb or LED (light-emitting diode) on the control panel when the turnout is thrown curved, and a green bulb or LED when it is moved to the straight position.

Some of Lionel's turnouts, the O Gauge 022 model previously referred to and the Postwar No. 1122 for O27 track, had built-in control rails which were connected to the solenoid terminals. Whenever an approaching locomotive's wheels bridged the gap between the ground and control rails, it caused the turnout to align itself with the correct route to prevent a derailment. Model 1121 does not have this safety feature, but it may be added easily.

One way is to wire the control rail of an approach track to the proper terminal to move the turnout rails in the appropriate direction. If the control rail is fairly lengthy, however, the solenoid will be powered for a long time, and may overheat. It will certainly be noisy, and since only a momentary shot of current is required, there are two better methods.

A small control rail can be provided in any track section by cutting through the rail an inch or two from the end and insulating it with plastic rail joiners. A wire is then run from this control rail to the appropriate terminal of the turnout, and any loco or car that runs over it will activate the solenoid.

Those who wish to avoid unnecessary breaks in the running rails (and I am one of them) can achieve the same effect by providing auxiliary contact strips. A piece of plated metal (I use coffee cans) is cut, drilled and shaped as shown in the photographs. A strip of masking tape is then fastened to the underside to serve as an insulator. This contact is screwed or bolted down next to the track so that the insulated portion rests on top of a running rail. A wire from it is connected to a turnout terminal. Whenever a set of wheels touches this strip, it is grounded and causes the turnout to operate.

I can vaguely remember a similar device attached to a 154 flashing railroad crossing signal that I used with my 1939 Lionel set. This arrangement was also provided with Marx crossing signals. Two U-shaped contacts about an inch long and each with a wire attached were snapped over one of the running rails. The wires were in turn connected to the outer two of three terminals on the Lionel 154 railroad crossing signal, and the center terminal was connected to the center rail. These U-shaped contacts were insulated on the underside to prevent grounding on the rail, but when a wheel passed over one, the circuit was completed, and one of the lights flashed.

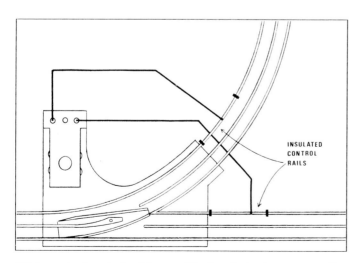

INSULATED
CONTROL
RAILS

Wiring a short control rail to one of the terminals of a turnout will cause that turnout to operate whenever a locomotive approaches from that direction. This principle was used on Lionel's 022 and 1122 non-derailing switches.

If the contacts were placed about 1½ inches apart, the wheels of the rolling stock would cause first one light, then the other, to

 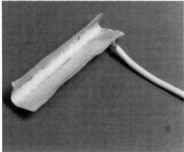 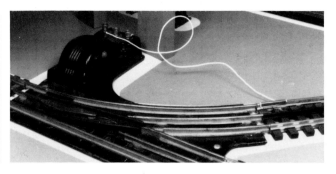

A simple metal contact plate made from a coffee can, with the underside insulated by a strip of masking tape as shown in the center photo, can serve to ground a turnout solenoid whenever touched by a set of wheels.

flash. The alternation was not entirely regular, depending upon the length of the cars in use, but it produced a pattern of flashing that was definitely superior to that generated by Lionel's 154 contactor. On our period layout, homemade U-shaped contacts or the same coffee-can plates which were applied to turnout control can be used in this application, as shown in the photograph.

Two Trains on One Track: Simple, Safe and Under Control

As the track plan in Chapter Three shows, my layout has four main line runs, all of them continuous loops. With no special wiring, this design allows for the simultaneous operation of four trains at once, without attention from the engineer. This provides lots of action, and usually impresses visitors with all the color, noise and lights, but the potential for even more fun is right there, awaiting only the addition of a simple device. We can increase those four trains to as many as nine. Three of the loops can each accommodate two trains at the same time; the longest loop allows us to run three!

The device in question is a 12-volt DC relay, equipped with a full-wave bridge rectifier. It's not expensive, comes with a plug-in socket that allows easy wiring, and permits two trains to

Two insulated contacts placed 1½ inches apart produce a relatively even rate of alternating flashes in a Lionel 154 highway crossing signal. This popular accessory was made both before and after the Second World War. Power may be supplied either by a wire from the third rail to the 154's center terminal, or by a lead from a fixed voltage post on the transformer that provides about 14 volts. The latter method ensures constant brilliance of the bulbs, independent of train speed. (Note: Highway flashers made by various companies may not always have the power terminal located in the center.)

follow each other on the same loop of track in absolute safety, without any manual adjustment of the throttle by the engineer.

The relay consists of a magnetic coil and a pair of movable spring-loaded arms that are normally touching a pair of contacts when at rest. When the coil is energized, it attracts a metal plate to which the flexible arms are connected, drawing them away from the first set of contacts and holding them against a second set. Power passing through these arms is thus transferred from one set of terminals to another whenever the relay is activated.

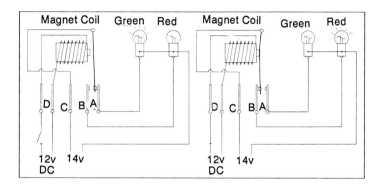

In this example of a DC relay application, power to light a bulb is supplied from the transformer to terminal C, as shown in the drawing at the left. A green bulb is wired to terminal A, and is lighted because the movable arm is resting against its contact point. When the magnetic coil receives 12 DC volts at terminal D, it pulls the contact arm to the position shown in the drawing on the right. Power now goes from terminal C through the arm to the contact attached to terminal B, lighting the red bulb and turning off the green one. (While just one set of contacts is shown for clarity, the relay actually has two, and can operate another set of two bulbs or perform other functions.)

The operation of the relay is simple. AC power from the transformer is fed into the full-wave bridge, where it is rectified into DC current and sent to the relay coil. This coil is then grounded to a control rail on the layout. When the relay is activated by a train touching the control rail, it transfers current from one set of contacts to another.

This device can be used to switch off the power to any section of track automatically. A 3-foot or longer track section is provided with fiber pins at both ends of the center power rail. Current to this isolated section is routed through the contacts of the relay that are normally closed, or touching each other. The magnetic coil of the relay is powered by the control rail of another section of track placed some distance ahead.

Imagine a slow train proceeding down the line, pursued by a faster one. The slow train reaches the section with the control rail as the one overtaking from behind comes into the section with the insulated third rail. The slow train triggers the relay through the control rail, and the contacts of the relay open, cutting off power to the faster train. This allows the slower one to move ahead, and by the time it is clear of the control rail and the relay is released to allow the faster train to proceed, the slower one has gained enough ground to be safe.

Since each relay has an unused set of contacts, a block signal such as Lionel's No. 153 can be wired to show green when there is no train on the control rail and power is reaching the third rail of the iso-

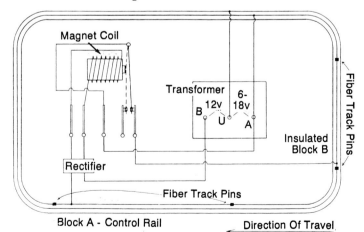

A slower train entering block A touches a control rail, activating the relay which then cuts off the power to the third rail of block B. Any train entering block B will stop, until block A is clear of traffic and the relay returns to its normal position.

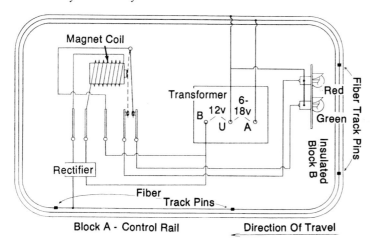

A Lionel 153 block signal wired to the second set of relay contacts will change from green to red when a train enters the block with the control rail. (For clarity, this diagram does not show the set of contacts which cuts off power to the track; this is illustrated in the previous drawing.)

lated section. When the block is occupied, the moving contact transfers the current to the red bulb, signifying no power in the third rail, in effect a "stop" signal.

Only one problem exists with this system. With power cut off from the third rail when the faster train reaches it, the engine's reverse unit will trip, and leave it standing in neutral when the current is restored. If the reverse unit is turned off (by moving the lever on top, inside the cab, or on the underside of the locomotive) it will continue moving in the same direction, but the reversing capability is then lost to the engineer until the lever is once again thrown.

There is a simple solution, however. If a lesser amount of current can be retained at the third rail of the isolated block, the reverse unit of any locomotive in the block will not trip. Depending upon the amount of current present, the loco can be made to slow down or come to a complete stop (stall), but the headlight will remain dimly lit, and progress will continue in the same direction when full power is restored. The engineer still retains full reverse capability when needed.

A resistor is placed between the relay contact attached to the third rail and the contact that is engaged when the relay is activated. Tripping the relay causes current to flow through the resistor before reaching the track, at reduced voltage, and the train slows down. The amount of resistance governs how much slower the locomotive will go. I use 1-ohm, 10-watt resistors connected in series. One or two will slow most locomotives enough to allow a train in the next block to gain some headway. Three or four will cause most locomotives to stall, but the trickle of current getting through will preserve the automatic reversing function.

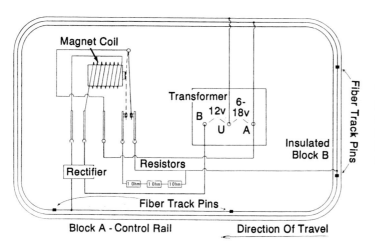

With the relay at rest as shown at left, current passes directly to the track. When the relay is energized, it passes first through the resistors and then to the track, causing any locomotive in the affected block to slow down or stall.

This method of block protection is much more realistic than simply cutting off the current. Locomotives slow down rather than die suddenly, and lights remain on.

It takes some experimentation to make this whole system of block protection function well. The distance between the isolated block and the control rail that triggers it will determine how safe the protected locomotive will be. Also, it is often advisable to use more than one control

A special socket allows easy connection or replacement of DC relays. Comparison of this photograph with the diagram on page 58 will reveal where the various leads are attached to the socket terminals.

rail section, to allow the slower train extra time to escape. On uphill grades, I wire the control rails all the way to the crest of the hill. It must also be remembered that both trains will run more slowly when both are receiving power; when one is stalled in the isolated block, the other receives more current and runs faster.

The amount of resistance introduced into the relay circuit will depend in part upon the characteristics of the locomotives in use, as some draw substantially more current than others. A compromise can usually be reached that will work with most equipment. One final word of caution: an on-off toggle switch should be wired into the power lead that goes to the relay coil, so that the system can be deactivated. Under certain conditions, the engineer may not wish to have power interrupted unexpectedly in the isolated blocks. On my panel, these toggles are coded green to prevent confusion with the red ones that turn on the track power.

In this age of electronic miracles, there are numerous solid state devices which can perform this function, and a host of other complex duties, to make model railroading both exciting and realistic. I have used some of them occasionally, such as circuits to operate the whistles and bells in Lionel tenders when their DC relays have failed. In general, however, I prefer to operate my period trains in a manner consistent with the years in which they were produced.

For those who, like me, prefer operational authenticity in their layouts, these relay systems for protecting two trains on one track were advocated in Lionel instruction books in the section dealing with the 153 block signal. Lionel called it "automatic train control," and described virtually the same method outlined above as well as a similar circuit involving their 153 track contactors, which were activated by the pressure of a passing train. (I can recall seeing this only in Postwar instruction booklets, however, so I guess I'm cheating just a bit, but these relays were available before the war.) Further information about wiring block signals can be found in Chapter Nine.

Now that we have track and power running to it, the time has come to consider what trains to run, and how to acquire them without taking out a second mortgage on the house.

SEVEN

Motive Power ~ America's Big Three

By far the largest number of toy trains ever produced by an American manufacturer before World War II came from the Lionel Corporation. These products were high in quality and durability, and possessed an appeal that guaranteed substantial sales figures even during all but the worst years of the Great Depression. Their toughness is legendary, and an amazing number of them can still be found.

Two other makers also enjoyed high volume sales, however: the Ives Corporation and American Flyer. Many of their products have survived, and provide a pleasant contrast to the familiar Lionel outlines, and hours of enjoyment for the collector-operator.

Sources of Author's Acquisitions

When I first abandoned HO scale for the new (to me) frontiers of antique toy trains, they seemed impossibly hard to find. A local antique dealer provided me with a battered but serviceable Postwar set with a 2037 locomotive and four chipped freight cars, and I had a clockwork Ives passenger set that had belonged to my father-in-law. Otherwise, Nova Scotia seemed to be a barren land for an aspiring enthusiast. Aside from a few inexpensive and battered Marx sets, my collection seemed to be going nowhere.

My first break came through a chance encounter at an auction on Nova Scotia's South Shore (which, by the way, is one of North America's most ruggedly beautiful landscapes). I successfully bid on some rusty Gargraves track and a few related items that I found dumped in a battered cardboard box, and this led me to a brief conversation with the auctioneer, who mentioned that he had some old Lionel trains stored away. He wanted to put them in his next auction, but had no idea of their value. He wondered if I would be willing to help him out.

Would I!

Armed with the latest Greenberg *Price Guide*, my wife Gay and I arrived at his home the following weekend, and walked into what was to my eyes a paradise, two tables filled with toys that I had only seen in books. There was a peacock-and-orange 253 passenger set, a string of 810-series freight cars, two sets of late-1930s coaches (600 series and 613 series), small

The author's most treasured train set was a gift from his father-in-law, Harold M. Bull, who as a child had received it in 1917. Consisting of an Ives 17 locomotive, 11 tender, 60 baggage and 61 chair car, the spring-wound motor still propels it at a brisk pace around its banked, two-rail sectional track. It rarely sees service on a layout, however, since clockwork trains cannot be controlled from a distance as electric ones can.

lithographed freight cars from the same period, and three steamers, not to mention lamp posts and signals of all kinds.

An hour later we had completed an inventory and produced a rough evaluation of the collection for the auctioneer, and Gay and I became the proud new owners of an orange Broadway and Main Street lamp post, a gift in return for our assistance in the cataloging process.

At the auction (to which I consigned my lowly Marx sets in hopes of some slight monetary return to offset intended purchases), there was some stiff competition. At that time, all of Nova Scotia boasted only about half a dozen toy train collectors, but they were all there, with bulging wallets. Despite visions of bankruptcy and debtor's prison flashing before my eyes, and with my Greenberg *Guide* clutched in my hand, I bravely bid and came away with the lovely little passenger set and the 810 freights, including a magnificent terra cotta crane.

The passing years and the experience they have brought me have shown that the prices I paid on that day were both reasonable and fair, but I didn't know it at the time. Clearly, if I were to pursue this hobby in a solvent manner, I needed information, lots of it.

About that time the TCA (Train Collectors Association) was running a series of advertisements in *Model Railroader* magazine, soliciting new members. I penned an inquiry and received information and a membership application form, which required me to obtain the support of two sponsors. After what must have been an exhaustive check on my suitability for membership and a probationary waiting period (I heard they even listed the time I played hooky from the second grade; those guys were thorough!), I received my permanent card.

Three other memberships followed: TTOS (Toy Train Operating Society), LCCA (Lionel Collectors Club of America) and LCAC (Lionel Collectors Association of Canada). With them came the next step in my education, their periodic newsletters full of interesting and informative articles. But I still had little success in finding trains in my own back yard, so I turned to an old friend, *Model Railroader*.

Under the listing "For Sale: O Tinplate" in that magazine's classified section, I discovered several dealers who circulated lists of trains for sale by mail. My experience with them was generally good, and I began to amass a small but satisfying roster of common, low-priced Prewar items, to some of which I applied my newly acquired restoration skills. This only whetted my appetite, however, and I decided that if I were going to join the mainstream of this hobby, I would have to travel.

My first train-buying trip was a two-day journey to the TTOS Convention in Rochester, New York, through the hottest weather outside of the Gobi Desert. Traveling to anywhere from Nova Scotia takes twice as long as from anyplace else, so I arrived road weary but expectant. My first sight of the trading hall confirmed the wisdom of making the trip; I was surrounded by a ballroom full of toy trains!

In spite of sore feet and an aching back (which I scarcely noticed until returning to my hotel room each night), I spent every possible moment on the trading floor, from opening bell to closing whistle. I bought a lot of trains, but even more important, I began to meet the publishers, dealers, parts suppliers, train meet organizers and fellow hobbyists that help to make train collecting so much fun. Despite my inexperience, they treated me with honesty and fairness, and I came away from that convention with toys, memories and a generally good feeling about the hobby. Even the folks at Canada Customs were gentle with me as I crossed the border, and my collection grew considerably at a reasonable cost that summer.

Since then I have attended, among others, a TCA Convention in Valley Forge, Pennsylvania, a Greenberg Auction in Timonium, Maryland, and the Grand-daddy of all train meets at York, Pennsylvania: seven big buildings full of every imaginable product of a dozen or more manufacturers. This latter trip raised my spirits high enough to survive even a disastrous head-on collision with a bear while traveling through the northern Maine woods on the way home. (That bear nearly outweighed my tiny Nissan Pulsar, but we escaped with minor damage. I didn't get out to ask the bear how he was feeling, leaving that risky encounter to the nearest available game warden.)

By now the reader will have noted my advocacy of the train meet as a prime source for acquiring new items. While the prices of toy trains are rising every year (along with the price of just about everything else!), these meets afford the opportunity to bargain-hunt and horse-trade, and to enjoy fellowship and a good time as well. The key to success is knowledge: one must become familiar with those key elements of rarity that contribute to the value of these toys, which include color variations, model numbers, factory errors, scarcity and aesthetic desirability, among others.

This knowledge can be acquired from a number of sources, such as the association newsletters and other publications. The TCA, for example, has recently released the second edition of their comprehensive book, *Lionel Trains, Standard of the World, 1900-1943* to members and to the general public. Greenberg Publishing Company produces volumes covering virtually every manufacturer of toy trains, and updates this material (including price guides) regularly. Tom McComas and James Tuohy have produced a six-volume set of books describing Lionel trains, advertising and archival history, and also publish a price guide and other specialties. A new magazine, *Classic Toy Trains*, provides collectors and operators with articles on a wide variety of subjects six times each year.

Primary sources are invaluable. These include original catalogs issued by the manufacturers, as well as advertising, dealer and service literature, instruction books and old magazines. Although original catalogs in good condition are usually quite expensive, Greenberg Publishing Company and others have issued reprints of all available Lionel catalogs (1902 to 1969) and many by Ives, American Flyer and other companies.

While the Maritime Federation of Model Railroaders holds annual conventions and regional meets in Atlantic Canada, these get-togethers are oriented more toward scale modelers, and only occasionally does one find tinplate items on the trading tables. Because of the restrictions of my work at Acadia University, and due to the time required for travel to meets and conventions in the United States, I continue to buy from dealers by mail, mostly with good success.

Collectors should expect to pay higher prices to dealers than they do at train meets. Those dealers who trade from full-service hobby shops have a considerable amount of overhead, and therefore the highest price tags, while the amounts charged by those for whom this business is either a sideline or a home-based enterprise will be somewhere in between.

This is not an unreasonable situation. Dealers are performing a service for collectors, and should be entitled to a reasonable markup for their efforts. When a dealer lists an item I especially want, but have been unable to find at meets, I am satisfied to pay an extra 10 to 30 percent for the convenience of having it sent directly to my home. When a dealer locates a piece that he knows I have been seeking, and takes the time to call me, that consideration is worth the higher price he may charge, provided his commission is not excessive.

My experience with such mail-order deals has been almost uniformly good, with only two cases of misrepresentation. Any hobby involving rarities and the exchange of a large amount of cash may be expected to attract its share of sharp dealers and outright crooks, but the associations work hard to maintain high standards among the membership. My advice is simple: get to know the people you deal with personally, be reasonable when making offers to buy (especially from dealers who make their living from finding these treasures for you), and pass the word if you encounter examples of deliberate misrepresentation.

My favorite source for toy trains, however, is other people's attics. Even in thinly populated Nova Scotia, old sets turn up with surprising regularity, and my wife and I read the classified section of the newspaper (specifically the "Articles For Sale" and "Antiques" columns) faithfully every day. Perhaps only once every two or three months does an appropriate ad appear, but we always track each one down. Frequently the prize is an old tin Marx set, or a scuffed and chipped plastic Alco locomotive from Lionel's period of decline in the 1960s. But sometimes, just sometimes, the goal is worth the chase.

This "Lioneltown" 137 station of Prewar origin turned up in a box of miscellaneous Marx tinplate, advertised in the columns of a Halifax newspaper and purchased for a very reasonable sum. The Marx items were traded away, but this station has a featured position on the author's layout. It contains a clever patented automatic stop device that brings trains to a halt for ten to twenty seconds to allow passengers to board or disembark, all without operator intervention.

One example of such a find is the pretty little 137 station shown in the photo above. Answering an ad in the paper, I traveled to Dartmouth, across the harbor from our capital city of Halifax, and found a cardboard box full of disreputable Marx tinplate from the 1950s that had apparently suffered the attentions of children with sumo wrestler tendencies. But tucked away in the bottom, scratched but miraculously undented, was this gem of Lionel's Prewar days, with its train control circuit still intact. It now provides scheduled stops daily for the trains on the elevated portion of my layout.

Word of mouth is another powerful tool. I have been fortunate in the generosity of friends who know of my passion for old trains, and who call to tell me of any possible lead. Often these prove fruitful. Equally helpful is my annual display in Denton Hall at Acadia University, in conjunction with our annual Christmas concert by my Acadia Concert Band.

Early in December of each year, the Band performs holiday music with an invited group from the community; in 1989, it was the exceptional 90-voice Wolfville School Choir, directed by Shelley Moore, a graduate of Acadia's School of Music. The seasonal selections are presented in a "Christmas morning" setting, with a fully decorated tree on stage and antique toys beneath it (dolls and blocks and teddy bears), surrounded by at least two operating train sets. These perform to the accompaniment of some appropriate composition, such as Sergei Prokofieff's "Train Ride."

In the lobby a substantial portion of my collection is displayed, as an example of Christmas toys from the past. It is gratifying to note the interest these trains arouse in the concert-goers. As a result, I have been privileged occasionally to assist someone in resurrecting a long-forgotten set from the attic in time for Christmas. It always pleases me to help give these toys a new lease on life, whether they remain with their original owners or are transferred to my collection. A toy train left in the attic is a sad waste; it was meant to be played with.

So let's find some to play with!

What Shall We Buy?

Choosing equipment for an operation-oriented layout differs somewhat from collecting for its own sake, wherein rarity and condition are often the primary considerations. When I buy a train for the shelf, I may seek obscure variations, pristine paint or original boxes, but the criteria are somewhat different when I'm looking for a locomotive to pull my tinplate coaches.

Performance, dependability and ease of restoration (when necessary) are my guidelines, much the same as if the target purchase were a used automobile. Several conditions may need to be fulfilled: what function will the piece of equipment be asked to perform, how will it look in relation to its surroundings and with its companion rolling stock, and can it be made to look good by an amateur like myself who lacks the skills of a master rebuilder of antiques?

The question of aesthetics is also an important one for me. The following suggestions are therefore a matter of taste and opinion, as my concept of an attractive locomotive may differ considerably from that of another collector. Nevertheless, and with temerity, I offer what I have learned from several years of searching for engines to pull my trains and (I hope) delight visitors to my layout.

Box Cab Electric Locomotives

I like electric-outline locomotives, sometimes called *box cab* electrics, and many are available at reasonable cost. I have a few from the earlier O Gauge period (c. 1915 to 1924), and tend to run them together for a convincing "antique" display. Lionel made them in two basic sizes, as represented by the 150 and 154 in the photograph below, formed from sheet metal and powered by primitive motors of simple design which can usually be put into running condition with relative ease.

These locomotives from Lionel's first decade of O Gauge production (1915-1924) are fairly plentiful at train meets, and their simple electric motors have proven to be durable. On a layout they convey both charm and atmosphere.

Those found in the best condition, of course, will command premium prices, but many serviceable units can be acquired for less and turned into showpieces with the investment of a few pleasant hours of painting and lettering, as described later in the chapter. Their simple motors rarely need more than cleaning and rewiring, and should parts be needed for repair (contact brushes, screws, pickup rollers and even armatures are available), they are easy to find at train meets or by mail order. Magazine advertisements and association newsletters are good sources for parts suppliers' names and addresses.

With its cast-iron body and sturdy motor, this Ives 3218 locomotive from the late 'teens was found in badly damaged but salvageable condition, and now provides a pleasant contrast when run with Lionel locomotives from the same era on the author's layout. Lettering for such projects is available in either decal or dry transfer form.

1. Lots of track and switches, a mixture of accessories of all sizes and a decidedly toylike atmosphere pervaded the author's previous Prewar layout, which enjoyed almost a full year's life span before giving way to his restless urge to build a better one.

2. Even Lionel's relatively small 33 Standard Gauge locomotive from the 'teens looks huge by comparison with one of the larger O Gauge sets from the same period, a 154 engine with 603-series cars.

3. *Ives produced some of the most attractively colored train sets of the 1920s, such as this red and black beauty in O Gauge.*

4. *Reliable Postwar Lionel motive power provides some collectors with the ultimate in operating fun and satisfaction.*

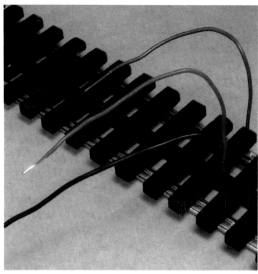

5. Although the massive 251 box cab electric is wider and 2½ inches longer than its little companion 248, they share the same short wheelbase. This results in severe clearance problems for the 251, as for any equipment with long overhanging ends.

6. Three wires are attached to each section of track. Black is the ground, red powers the third rail, and green is the control for accessories and relays.

7. With their bright enamel and brass trim, box cab electric locomotives from the late 1920s and early '30s make a showy display when operating on a layout. Their dependable mechanisms make for consistent operation, but it is often wise to install an electrical bypass to defeat the sometimes sporadic functioning of early reverse units during automatic operation.

8. *Toy trains are beautiful, as illustrated by American Flyer's large and small versions of the Milwaukee Road's "Hiawatha."*

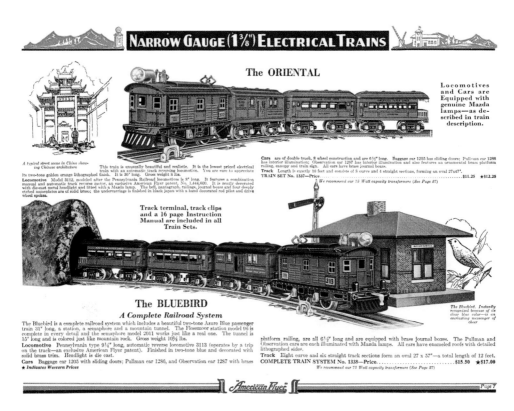

9. *Pictured in the 1929 American Flyer catalog, the 3113 Bluebird came with a detail-packed lithographed body, showing stripes and rivets in contrasting yellow. This method of decorating toy trains was beautiful but susceptible to scratching and fading, and cannot be authentically restored.*

10. While not as detailed as the original lithography, the enameled finish on this 3013 Bluebird, with striping of artist's tape applied to imitate the factory design, is a fair approximation.

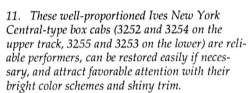

11. These well-proportioned Ives New York Central-type box cabs (3252 and 3254 on the upper track, 3255 and 3253 on the lower) are reliable performers, can be restored easily if necessary, and attract favorable attention with their bright color schemes and shiny trim.

12. Each of these Lionel box cab electrics is a good performer. The smaller 248 and 252 models (upper track) came in a wide variety of colors, making them fun for the collector to search out. The mid-sized 253 New Haven style and the rounded 254 St. Paul type were also produced in many colors, but the big 251 came only in red or gray.

13. A Lionel 262 painted in Blue Comet colors makes a fair O Gauge imitation of the Standard Gauge 390 that headed the larger Blue Comet set in its first year of production.

14. A silver 262 seems right at home (if a shade ostentatious) leading a train of silver-roofed passenger cars. Such custom restorations make good use of damaged equipment that might otherwise be ignored.

15. *Reliable performers and attractive in design, American Flyer's mid-priced locomotives such as this 422 and custom-finished red 3308 had innovative features such as the latter's ringing bell.*

16. *Lionel's 1668 and 238 interpretations of the Pennsylvania Torpedo streamlined steam locomotive are excellen' choices for operation. The 238 seen here was found in poor condition, and was customized in a two-tone paint scheme to highlight the well-detailed boiler casting.*

17. Headed by a 264E Commodore Vanderbilt streamlined steamer, the Red Comet with its short 603/604 coaches makes an attractive if not too realistic set, and is an excellent performer. The similar 265E looks good with a string of streamlined cars borrowed from the Flying Yankee, as illustrated by this relatively rare Blue Streak set.

18. Presenting a fairly accurate representation of the Union Pacific original, Lionel's City of Denver set (lower track) whistled, reversed and lit up a child's railroad in spectacular fashion. Thanks to its quality construction, it can still do so today. American Flyer's interpretation of the same prototype is crossing the upper trestle.

19. Power to light the cars of Flyer's streamlined passenger sets was transmitted from the locomotive through springy contacts that mated when the vestibules were connected, as shown in this sleek City of Denver. The foot-long cars contributed a realistic appearance to this well-made model.

20. This big Lionel 251 box cab electric is much more attractive with a lighted cab, making the unlighted 254 beside it almost drab by c[ ] When installed following the author's suggestions, these lights and the glazing in the windows do nothing to reduce the value of locomo[ ] can be removed at any time without leaving a trace.

21.   *These four 9½-inch American Flyer cars date from 1939, and have the newer automatic latch couplers, which could not mate with earlier designs: 407 sand car (gondola), 408 boxcar, 412 milk car and 415 floodlight car.*

22.   *These small Lionel freight cars of the '30s represent various stages in the development of the 650 series. The 656 stock car is similar to its four-wheeled predecessor, and has latch couplers. One 2654 tanker has nickel plates and early automatic couplers with large ribbed-top boxes, while the other is a later version with decals; both share the body from the earlier 804. Note the smaller coupler box on the second tank car, an improved design introduced in 1940.*

23. *Lionel's popular 810 crane had a relatively subdued paint job when introduced in 1930 (foreground), but turned bright five years later (left). Although quite expensive at the time, this car was a good seller, since children could do a lot with its hand-operated mechanisms. But it took a powerful locomotive to move it around the layout, and the big boom needed a lot of clearance through the tunnels.*

24. *Lionel's premium-priced cars of the early '30s had a long life span, being offered in a variety of colors through 1942. The larger 613, 614 and 615 were included in the O Gauge Blue Comet Set. The 600 group came three ways (gray with red roofs, all red, and blue and silver) but not in the custom gray and black shown; maybe Mr. Cowen missed a good combination here!*

25.   *These long and handsome Ives 129-series cars boasted well-detailed lithography plus interior lights and glazed windows. Their proportions were good, and they were often sold in sets with matching box cab locos. The house in the foreground is a Lionel 189 villa.*

26.   *Both clockwork and electric American Flyer sets were sold in Canada with either these Canadian National cars or similar ones lettered "Canadian Pacific". Few can be found today in good condition. The coaches measure 5½ inches over the frame ends, and larger 6½-inch versions were also made.*

27. During its final two years as an independent company, Ives produced enameled passenger cars painted in unusual and attractive color schemes and with brass trim. They were often packaged with box cab electric locomotives decorated to match.

28. A few hours of pleasant work will return battered toy trains to Like New condition, making them assets to any display layout.

29. Lionel revolutionized the toy train industry just prior to World War II with four massive motorized accessories that gave young engineers far more to do than simply run the trains. Dominating a layout by their size and action, three of them load coal, logs and scrap metal, while the bascule bridge rises majestically into the air to allow the tallest yachts to pass beneath.

A BEAUTIFUL NEW LIONEL STATION—COMPLETELY ILLUMINATED

An Attractive Addition to a Lionel Railroad

NO. 128—This elaborate new station is just what Lionel users have long desired. It is up to date in every detail. The station is mounted on a terrace which contains beautifully landscaped flower beds. In the center bravely floats an American flag mounted on a tall flagstaff. A beautifully designed stairway leads from the ground to the terrace. The retaining wall surrounding the structure represents ornamental masonry. The station is illuminated inside and out by electric bulbs, and beautifully designed torches illuminate the terrace. The building is equipped with swinging doors and other characteristic Lionel features. The roof is removable so that the electric fixture in the interior can easily be reached. This elaborate station is made entirely of heavy steel, beautifully enameled and decorated. It is 31½ inches long, 18 inches deep and 12 inches high.

Code Word "YEN."

No. 129 Station Platform

THIS platform is the same as the one described above, and is listed separately so that owners of Lionel Stations Nos. 124, 122 and 121 can make use of them in this most elaborate setting, which so greatly adds to the appearance of the entire railroad layout.

Code Word "YIELD."

Prices are Listed on Page 45

36

30. *Although the 1929 Lionel catalog didn't say so, this 124 station and 129 platform combination, collectively No. 128, was suitable only for Standard Gauge trains, being far too large to look right on an O Gauge layout.*

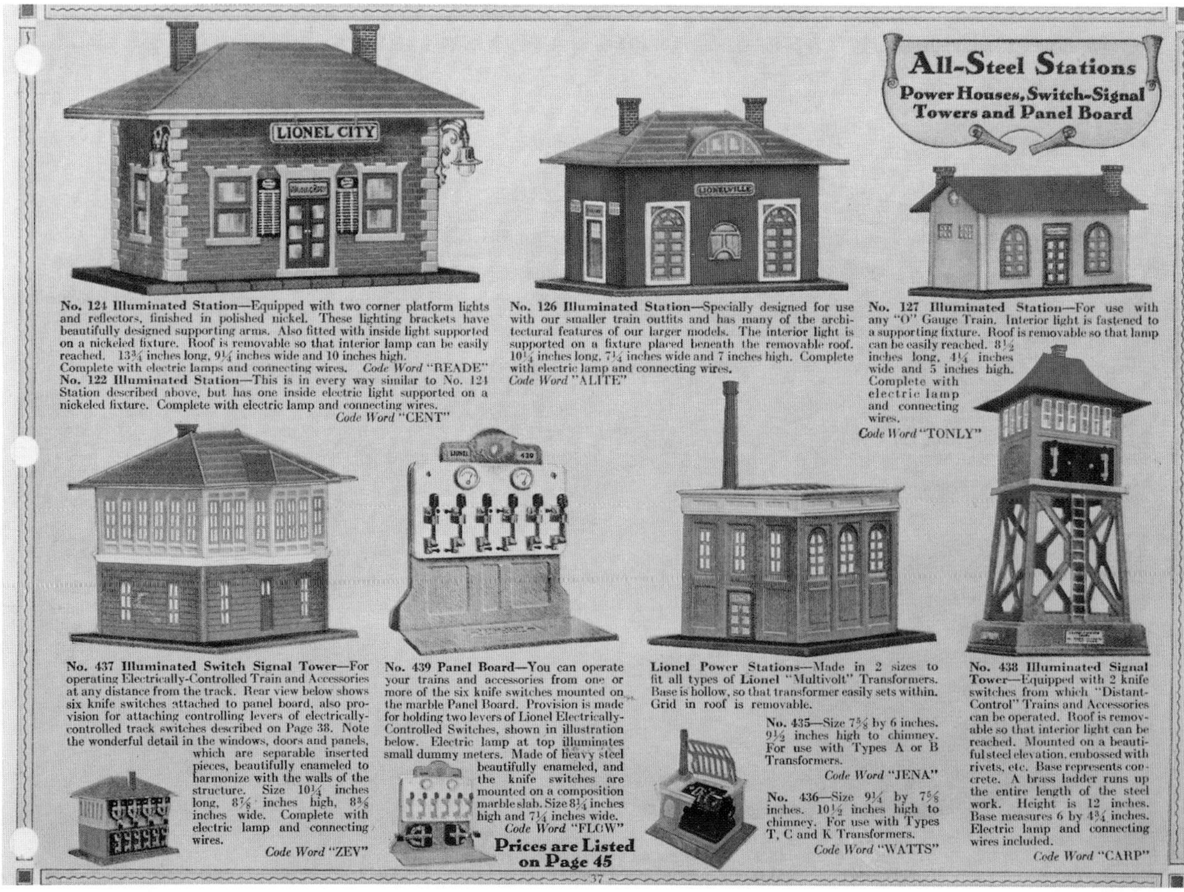

All-Steel Stations
Power Houses, Switch-Signal Towers and Panel Board

No. 124 Illuminated Station—Equipped with two corner platform lights and reflectors, finished in polished nickel. These lighting brackets have beautifully designed supporting arms. Also fitted with inside light supported on a nickeled fixture. Roof is removable so that interior lamp can be easily reached. 13¾ inches long, 9¼ inches wide and 10 inches high. Complete with electric lamps and connecting wires. *Code Word* "READE"

No. 122 Illuminated Station—This is in every way similar to No. 124 Station described above, but has one inside electric light supported on a nickeled fixture. Complete with electric lamp and connecting wires. *Code Word* "CENT"

No. 126 Illuminated Station—Specially designed for use with our smaller train outfits and has many of the architectural features of our larger models. The interior light is supported on a fixture placed beneath the removable roof. 10¼ inches long, 7¼ inches wide and 7 inches high. Complete with electric lamp and connecting wires. *Code Word* "ALITE"

No. 127 Illuminated Station—For use with any "O" Gauge Train. Interior light is fastened to a supporting fixture. Roof is removable so that lamp can be easily reached. 8½ inches long, 4¼ inches wide and 5 inches high. Complete with electric lamp and connecting wires. *Code Word* "TONLY"

No. 437 Illuminated Switch Signal Tower—For operating Electrically-Controlled Train and Accessories at any distance from the track. Rear view below shows six knife switches attached to panel board, also provision for attaching controlling levers of electrically-controlled track switches described on Page 38. Note the wonderful detail in the windows, doors and panels, which are separable inserted pieces, beautifully enameled to harmonize with the walls of the structure. Size 10¼ inches long, 8⅞ inches high, 8⅜ inches wide. Complete with electric lamp and connecting wires. *Code Word* "ZEV"

No. 439 Panel Board—You can operate your trains and accessories from one or more of the six knife switches mounted on the marble Panel Board. Provision is made for holding two levers of Lionel Electrically-Controlled Switches, shown in illustration below. Electric lamp at top illuminates small dummy meters. Made of heavy steel beautifully enameled, and the knife switches are mounted on a composition marble slab. Size 8¼ inches high and 7¼ inches wide. *Code Word* "FLOW"

Lionel Power Stations—Made in 2 sizes to fit all types of **Lionel** "Multivolt" Transformers. Base is hollow, so that transformer easily sets within. Grid in roof is removable.

No. 435—Size 7⅝ by 6 inches. 9½ inches high to chimney. For use with Types A or B Transformers. *Code Word* "JENA"

No. 436—Size 9¼ by 7⅝ inches. 10½ inches high to chimney. For use with Types T, C and K Transformers. *Code Word* "WATTS"

No. 438 Illuminated Signal Tower—Equipped with 2 knife switches from which "Distant-Control" Trains and Accessories can be operated. Roof is removable so that interior light can be reached. Mounted on a beautiful steel elevation, embossed with rivets, etc. Base represents concrete. A brass ladder runs up the entire length of the steel work. Height is 12 inches. Base measures 6 by 4¾ inches. Electric lamp and connecting wires included. *Code Word* "CARP"

Prices are Listed on Page 45

37

31. *Pictured side by side, the 124, 126 and 127 stations in the 1929 Lionel catalog display their disparate sizes. The 124 appeared much bigger in proportion than it actually was, probably as a sales technique to entice buyers to spend the extra $4.25 (total $9.50) that it cost, compared with the 126. These accessories were not cheap, even in 1929 dollars; the 126 sold for $4.75, and the 127 for $3.10. Much of the cost of the 124 went into the ornate light fixtures; a similar 122 without them sold for $3 less.*

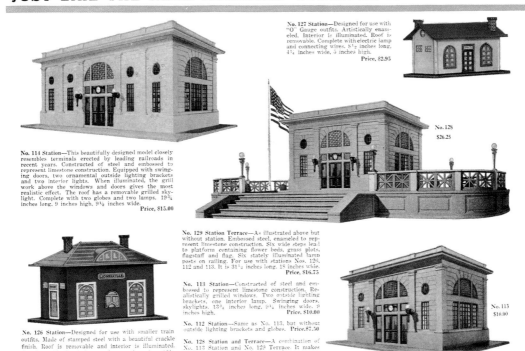

No. 127 Station—Designed for use with "O" Gauge outfits. Artistically enameled. Interior is illuminated. Roof is removable. Complete with electric lamp and connecting wires. 8½ inches long, 4¼ inches wide, 5 inches high.
Price, $2.95

No. 114 Station—This beautifully designed model closely resembles terminals erected by leading railroads in recent years. Constructed of steel and embossed to represent limestone construction. Equipped with swinging doors, two ornamental outside lighting brackets and two interior lights. When illuminated, the grill work above the windows and doors gives the most realistic effect. The roof has a removable grilled skylight. Complete with two globes and two lamps. 19¾ inches long, 9 inches high, 9½ inches wide.
Price, $15.00

No. 128
$26.25

No. 129 Station Terrace—As illustrated above but without station. Embossed steel, enameled to represent limestone construction. Six wide steps lead to platform containing flower beds, grass plots, flagstaff and flag. Six stately illuminated lamp posts on railing. For use with stations Nos. 126, 112 and 113. It is 31½ inches long, 18 inches wide.
Price, $16.75

No. 113 Station—Constructed of steel and embossed to represent limestone construction. Realistically grilled windows. Two outside lighting brackets, one interior lamp. Swinging doors, skylights. 13¾ inches long, 9¾ inches wide, 9 inches high.
Price, $10.00

No. 112 Station—Same as No. 113, but without outside lighting brackets and globes. Price, $7.50

No. 128 Station and Terrace—A combination of No. 113 Station and No. 129 Terrace. It makes an impressive sight and gives majesty to your Railroad.
Price, $26.25

No. 126 Station—Designed for use with smaller train outfits. Made of stamped steel with a beautiful crackle finish. Roof is removable and interior is illuminated. Complete with electric lamp and connecting wires. 10¼ inches long, 7¼ inches wide, 7 inches high. Price, $4.75

No. 113
$10.00

[Page Thirty-four]

32. *The 1932 Canadian edition of Lionel's catalog displays stations on page 34, and features the big urban 112 and 114 models. The 114 is pictured as mounted on the 129 terrace first built for use with the 124 type. Thanks to import duties and the dollar exchange, the cost to Canadians was $18 for the 113 and $27.50 for the 114 at the height of the Depression. It's easy to understand why the author has yet to find one in his home province of Nova Scotia.*

33. *A tan base coat allows "dirt" to show through the green grass paint wherever the surface of the foam is not touched by the brush. Rock effects are added with gray paint, applied with a nearly dry and relatively stiff brush passed horizontally over the surface. (Mickey Mouse stokes the firebox as his circus comes to town on the upper track. This rare 1936 set was acquired at a country auction just one day before the final photos were taken for this book.)*

34. With their bright colors, massive proportions and non-stop action, Prewar trains and accessories are at their best in a toylike setting, delighting the eye and stimulating the imagination of all who would remain forever young.

Ives locomotives from the same period are usually made of cast iron, such as the 3218 pictured here. They are often found with parts broken off; pilots and pantographs are the most vulnerable. But the hobby is fortunate to have adherents who manufacture replacements for nearly every model, and their names appear in the directories of the various collectors' associations. For the most part, they run their cottage industries as a sideline; their volume is not high, and I am amazed at how reasonable their prices usually are.

Other hobbyists serve the same function as an auto salvage yard, collecting and disassembling damaged and unrestorable trains and selling those parts which are still useful. Such suppliers often advertise in the classified sections of hobby magazines, and I have found them to be very helpful in seeking out parts I need.

Locomotives from this early period can hardly be described as smooth runners, however. Loose manufacturing tolerances in the motor parts and the inevitable wear that seven decades can bring will often result in somewhat erratic behavior on the track: a wobble or lurch is not uncommon. Furthermore, some were equipped with but one roller pickup, such as the Ives 3218, and these can easily stall at turnouts and crossings, or even on dirty track at slow speeds.

Nevertheless I run them frequently, but not in complex situations with more than one train on a loop, or in automatic stop-and-go situations. These early items are at their best when operated in a continuous fashion at moderate speeds, and under the watchful eye of the engineer.

Beginning about 1925, however, these toys improved markedly. Lionel introduced a second generation of O Gauge locos which were made in great numbers, colorfully painted, sturdily built and equipped with excellent motors. Ives switched from cast-iron to tinplate bodies, and American Flyer offered a wide range of box cab electrics in both painted and lithographed steel. Automatic reverse units were introduced, beginning with the superior Ives drum type with forward-neutral-reverse positions in 1925. A half-dozen or more of these reliable units performing on a period layout is a beautiful sight. See color photo 7.

American Flyer sold the "Mutt and Jeff" of the toy train world in the '20s: the tiny 1096, and the massive 3020 with four-wheel leading and trailing trucks. The latter was a very realistic representation of the big New York Central T-type urban locomotives in use at that time on the East Coast, and ran well. Despite their positions at opposite ends of the price list, these two models had exactly the same electric motor powering them, a reliable unit that ran at low voltage.

The largest and smallest of American Flyer's box cab electrics were powered by the same motor. This tiny 1096 was found caked with mud and sand after spending several neglected years outdoors, but some new wiring and a thorough cleaning made it run again. Both of these locos were badly rusted, but enough of the original tinplate bodies survived to allow complete restoration. The large 3020 originally had a track-trip reverse unit, which was removed for reasons explained in the text.

Many of American Flyer's locomotives came equipped with a track-trip reverse unit, consisting of an angled metal bar that projected from either side. A trackside lever could be set to contact this bar when the locomotive passed, reversing the engine and sending it off in the opposite direction. This was a poor substitute for the Ives and Lionel units which could be controlled from the transformer, but it worked. Unfortunately, these projecting bars tend to catch on switches, station platforms and accessories on the layout, and I normally remove them, and replace them with a modern E-unit (automatic reverse) or manual reverse switch. (As always with such modifications, the original parts should be saved for reinstallation, in case the owner should want to restore the locomotive to its original factory condition.)

Flyer also made many different box cabs with lithographed bodies, but I usually avoid them unless they are in excellent condition (in which case the price is normally high). It is nearly impossible to restore scratched or faded lithography, and shabby locomotives are not welcome at my operating sessions. To simulate the lithographed finish with enamel and hand-applied artwork is tedious and not entirely satisfying, as the result rarely resembles the original accurately, but I have restored two such engines: a tiny Hiawatha seen in the background of color photo 8, and a 3013 Bluebird made in 1927.

Color photo 9 shows a similar 3113 Bluebird as pictured in the 1929 catalog, lithographed with yellow stripes, rivets and window frames. It was an attractive design, but six decades after its manufacture the finish is often scratched, and a variety of conditions (including especially sunlight) can also cause fading. Because I like the overall proportions of this New Haven-style engine, I attempted to duplicate the factory finish on my 3013 Bluebird with enamel and ⅟32-inch yellow LetraLine flexible artist's tape. The results were pleasing enough to me that I operate this engine frequently, but its just isn't the same as the original. See color photo 10.

There are several other styles of box cab locomotives that were produced by American Flyer, many distinguished mainly by their unattractiveness. A steeple cab design bearing numbers such as 1218 looked foreshortened and crude, with its oversized handrails and lack of trim, but it sold in surprising numbers and runs well. A big St. Paul electric looks all right when mounted on a long frame, but in the configuration shown in the photo below, with flattened pilots just below the body shell, it looks awkward and cumbersome. Despite its string of matching passenger cars, I rarely run it.

Stubby and high above the rails, American Flyer's 3116 St. Paul electric-type locomotive is neither graceful nor attractive. Although it runs satisfactorily, its inherent unattractiveness in the eyes of many may keep it off the layout.

Ives made several models of New York Central box cabs in two basic sizes on different size frames during the 1920s. They are strong performers, and even the fragile drum-type automatic reverse units can often be made to work again (although I usually replace them with modern E-units for reliability when operating). See color photos 11 and 12.

Lionel made six different sizes of box cab electrics, and I run all except the largest (the twin-motored, twin-pantographed monster 256 that won't go through my tunnels or bridges, and costs a fortune at most train meets besides). They all run well, with the exception of their notorious automatic reverse units.

Ives held a secure patent on the drum-type reverse unit, and Lionel's pendulum-style imitation lacked a neutral position. The latter consisted of a pair of swiveling fiber strips containing sets of electrical contacts, suspended from a fulcrum. A solenoid was positioned so that the application of current moved a bar which pushed this pendulum to one side, engaging two of the contacts. Any interruption of the current cycled the solenoid, causing it to move the pendulum in the opposite direction, realigning the contacts to reverse the current to the brushes.

Unless absolutely reliable electrical contact can be maintained, these locomotives are prone to sudden reversals of direction. It is often humorous but potentially destructive to watch these engines screech to a halt and gallop off the other way. Although I have managed to coax a couple of these pendulums to perform with some dependability, I usually replace them with modern E-units. (My wife says I'm a killjoy!)

The majority of O Gauge toy trains built prior to 1930 were of electric-outline configuration, with the notable exception of some tiny Ives and American Flyer cast-iron steamers, which were actually just clockwork products with electric motors substituted. Box cab locos were easier and cheaper to build than the more complex steamers, and since the largest toy train market was in the eastern United States, where this type of engine was common, sales were brisk.

Lionel had built steamers in Standard Gauge from 1906 through 1923, toylike caricatures based on no specific prototype, but dropped them from the line when their more realistic box cabs were designed. The next steamer the firm introduced was the massive Standard Gauge 390 in 1929, hardly scale but much closer in appearance to a real locomotive than the earlier products had been. Up to this point, Lionel had yet to produce a steam locomotive in O Gauge.

Steam Locomotives

This changed in 1930 with the introduction of two new models, the large 260E and its comparatively tiny companion, the 257/8. Sold as a premium product throughout its life span, the 260E had a cast frame and sheet metal construction, and was accompanied by a Vanderbilt-style oil tender which rode on huge Standard Gauge wheels. During the first year of production, the 260E's pendulum reverse unit could not be turned off, making it an unpredictable performer. This fault was corrected the following year by the inclusion of an on-off switch in the cab.

The 260E looks great on a layout. Its firebox glows red, and it makes a satisfying clatter over the rail joints, thanks to its considerable weight. I have substituted O Gauge wheels on the tender to minimize problems when it passes through switches, but have made no other changes. Even the original pendulum reverse unit continues to function in a dependable manner. This engine came with the firm's largest freight cars, and also in uncataloged sets with a set of huge red passenger cars, the 710 series; it's a magnificent sight when under way.

The much smaller 257 was intended for the low-priced end of the market and was non-reversing, although the otherwise identical model 258 had a hand-operated reverse lever in the cab. The loco shown in the photo has original 257 plates, but also has a reverse lever, indicating that Lionel may not have been overly scrupulous in matching catalog numbers to features.

This baby steamer is also a fine runner, and imparts a very satisfying toylike appearance when towing a string of 800-series four-wheeled freight cars or the smallest 529-type coaches. It has sufficient weight to enable it to climb hills well with three or four cars, and its fat, exposed headlight bulb attracts a lot of attention, especially when emerging from a tunnel.

The largest and smallest of Lionel's early toylike O Gauge steamers were both introduced in 1930. The big 260E would continue for years, being updated and modernized as the 255E and 263E later in the decade, but the little 257/8 would be dropped from the catalog after only one year, although it was available through 1932.

Probably the most common engine of this era was the 262 model, introduced in 1931. It progressed through various stages of brass, copper and nickel trim, had an automatic reverse when sold as a 262E, and was well-engineered and durable. Its basic shell was updated in the mid-'30s with less toylike wheels and marker lights in place of flags. A similar model was introduced in 1936, numbered "249". In all its forms this design proved to be a strong performer, and it was made in vast numbers, although specimens in excellent condition command premium prices today.

These mid-sized steamers were among Lionel's biggest sellers in the 1930s, heading a bewildering variety of freight and passenger sets. The black 262E (right) and gun metal 249E were not very prototypical in design, but had a lot of charm and appeal. These mid-'30s versions illustrate Lionel's gradual movement away from a toylike appearance, with more realistic trim such as sand pipes that terminate in the correct location in front of the drivers. The tender of the 249E contains a remote-control whistle.

These engines are frequently found in very poor condition, and I cannot resist customizing such wrecks. They lend themselves to a wonderfully wide range of interpretation. For example, Lionel's justly famous Standard Gauge Blue Comet had an O Gauge counterpart, a string of 613-series coaches headed by a large 263E locomotive in two-tone blue. This set is highly sought after by collectors, but I have never liked its appearance, as the cars seem too small in comparison with the locomotive.

The first Standard Gauge Blue Comet was headed not by the famous and massive 4-4-4 steamer numbered "400", but by a more modest 390 2-4-2. This locomotive bears a close resemblance to the O Gauge 262, which to my eye is in much better proportion to the 613-series passenger coaches. Having found a near-basket case 262, I decided to recreate the spirit of that early 390 set in O Gauge, and restored it in two-tone blue with a cream stripe. As far as Lionel history is concerned, this locomotive is a "never-was," but I like it (and that's what a hobby should be all about: personal satisfaction!). See color photo 13.

Another battered 262 made its way to my doorstep, and sat around for months with its pilot broken off, frame cracked in numerous places, cab squeezed out of shape and rust on every surface. I couldn't work up much enthusiasm for restoring it; after all, how many black 262s does one need? Then one day I found myself searching for just the right loco to pull my long and lean 1685-series passenger cars. Decorated in blue with silver roofs, these cars look fine behind a gray 249 or black 262, but something more spectacular was in order, and my attention turned to the disreputable old 262.

The results can be seen in color photo 14. Joshua Lionel Cowen would probably not have approved, but this silver 262 commands a lot of attention. It's perhaps a bit gaudy, but not really out of place as a product of the company that produced the infamous pink girls' train of 1957. Cowen had lapses in good taste, too!

This 263E was the last and largest of Lionel's sheet me locos of the 1930s, and stayed in the catalog through 1939. Replaced by the more prototypical die-cast models before the war, this engine was premium priced and produced in fewer numbers than the common 262 and 249. It commands high prices in today's collector market.

In 1936 Lionel revised its large 260E steamer, giving it more realistic wheels, nickel trim, marker lights instead of flag holders, and a sleek Vanderbilt tender with a remote-control whistle. Renumbered 263E, this loco came in gun metal or two-tone blue (for the Blue Comet set), and looks best at the head of a string of large 810-series freight cars. With its drum-type E-unit and powerful motor, it is an excellent performer.

Another Lionel engine available in large numbers is the 259E, along with its similar and slightly cheaper companion 258 (a different locomotive from the model introduced in 1930). These small sheet metal locomotives powered the lowest-priced O Gauge sets, and while they do not perform as well as the larger units with their greater weight, they are adequate, if not exciting.

Collectors are usually pleased to find tiny 1661E or 1681E Lionel Juniors, some of which originally came with the Ives name on the tender. I recommend keeping these cute little items on the shelf, however; trying to keep them running reliably is possible but unrewarding, as they need constant attention.

Lionel began courting the scale model market with the 1937 introduction of a magnificent Hudson, the famous 700E. Gradually phasing out earlier toy designs, the company introduced four sizes of smaller die-cast locomotives in varying price ranges, and several sizes of scale and semi-scale switchers. These closely resembled real engines, and some were continued after the war. While they are excellent runners, their similarity to Postwar designs does not provide the antique atmosphere I seek for my Prewar layout, so I keep them on the shelf. They have great attraction for many operators, however, as their mechanisms and reverse units are highly reliable, and they shuffle the clever operating freight cars with ease.

By the early '30s, the bankrupt Ives Corporation had been absorbed and finally discontinued by Lionel, but American Flyer weathered the economic storms and produced a substantial number of steamers. While Flyer used about a dozen and a half different body shell castings or stampings, they can be divided roughly into three categories (small, medium and large) with somewhat similar characteristics within each group. Those with streamlined body shells will be discussed later in the chapter.

Early American Flyer steam locomotive designs had cast-iron boilers, but these did not last much beyond the turn of the decade. In 1931 a long and graceful model numbered 3302 appeared, a long-wheelbase 2-4-2 with detailed valve gear, glowing red light in the firebox and a substantial Vanderbilt tender. This design was altered and improved in various ways through 1937, and carried many different catalog numbers, such as the 3326 pictured here.

Many innovative features were incorporated, including a ringing bell and automatic reversing, but the latter was not uniformly successful. In trying to circumvent the Ives patent on the drum-type E-unit, American Flyer experimented with a number of schemes to get their locos to back up by remote control, and most of these large 2-4-2s contained one of the weirdest, an electro-mechanical arrangement attached by a cumbersome series of levers to the drive wheels.

This system engaged a gear mechanism when the motor stopped turning the wheels, causing the levers to realign the electrical contacts.

It worked fine if current was interrupted while the loco was moving at a good rate of speed, but a leisurely pace would often result in the unit stalling before the levers completed their cycle. Patient tinkering and lubrication will improve the situation somewhat, but it isn't completely reliable and lacks a neutral position. Later locomotives with this device can be identified by the lever protruding from the boiler just in front of the cab; the highest position indicates reverse. There is a lockout lever behind the rear driver on the right-hand side to disable the automatic reversing feature.

Large and graceful steam locomotives pulled American Flyer's large series of freight and passenger cars in the early 1930s. They were made in large numbers and their sturdy construction has insured a high survival rate. Note the protruding reverse-unit lever just forward of the cab roof.

I personally like this engine, and run it frequently. It isn't as smooth an operator as my Lionels, but it has lots of power and a nice appearance that successfully combines a satisfactory amount of realism with a definite "toy" flavor.

Flyer's mid-sized locos, like the 422 from 1939 pictured here, were also good, strong pullers, and this model had a vastly improved drum-type reverse unit with a neutral position, very similar to Lionel's. It looks good pulling either 9½- or 6½-inch freight cars, or any of the small or mid-sized passenger cars, and is still readily available in large numbers at reasonable prices. Like the Lionel 262, it is often found in poor condition, and therefore serves me well for custom finishes such as on the red 3308 of similar design shown in color photo 15.

This model had Flyer's interesting bell-ringer mechanism, a solenoid-operated device triggered by a stud on one of the driving wheels. This stud grounded the solenoid each time the wheel revolved, causing a rod to strike a small bell mounted in the cab. It's fussy to adjust, but functions very well and sounds good, although its rapid rate of ringing is not very prototypical. There is a defeat switch located in the cab; those bells can get on one's nerves!

Throughout the 1930s, American Flyer produced a huge number of small steamers with sheet metal bodies and 2-4-0 or 2-4-4 wheel arrangements. They are short, top-heavy and somewhat cute in appearance, but often run erratically, as they are light in weight and their mechanisms are not highly refined. The several examples I own are noisy and difficult to operate smoothly, but I run them often. They make little pretense toward realism, especially when hitched to tiny four-wheeled coaches as shown in the top photo on the next page, and to me they represent the essence of the Depression-era toy train.

Some of these small locos had whistles mounted in the cabs, operated by a gear arrangement connected to a rear driver. They blew at regular intervals as the train circled the track, and are rarely found in working condition today; I suspect many were deliberately disabled by exasperated parents seeking aural relief!

This Chicago-based company was not nearly as well organized in cataloging its products as Lionel, and many different numbers were assigned to these locos. In addition, many were uncataloged and bore no numbers at all; these are hard to identify today. Consequently the whole series is often referred to as "Type 10" or "Type 403" (after one identifiable model) for convenience.

Many low-priced Flyer locos such as this one present a special problem for operators. The oversized gears on the drive wheels catch on or ride up over turnout guardrails. Since I like to run these cute steamers on my layout, they have dictated my use of Lionel 1121 turnouts, through which they can pass with ease. A further description of this problem appears in Chapter Five.

Short and ugly-cute, these little sheet metal steamers were made in huge numbers by American Flyer in the '30s, and sold for very low prices with small and simple freight or passenger sets. The coach and observation car in this set contain lights, an uncommon feature in such low-priced products.

During the second half of the decade, which included the A. C. Gilbert takeover of the firm, American Flyer released several new locomotive designs that may be of interest to operators as well as collectors. The large Hudson that came out in 1936 was not scaled as accurately as Lionel's 700E which appeared a year later, but it required no special track, represented a definite departure from the "toy" look, and cost $60 less than the 700E's $75 price tag. The Flyer Hudson was the first six-drivered O Gauge locomotive mass-produced by a major American manufacturer.

A smaller six-driver chassis was made starting in 1938, and powered a 4-6-2 Pacific, a 2-6-4 and a handsome 0-6-0 switcher. This mechanism is geared low and runs well at slow speeds, an especially valued feature in the switcher.

Based on a slow-running six-drivered chassis, these American Flyer designs (429 switcher and 427 2-6-4) were added to the line about the time of A. C. Gilbert's purchase of the company. They were among the last of the large Flyer locos, soon giving way to smaller 3/16-inch-to-the-foot scale models that formed the foundation of the firm's Postwar S Gauge conversion.

Streamlined Steam Locomotives

Both Lionel and Flyer were quick to follow the example of prototype railroads in the mid-1930s by producing models of such streamlined locomotives as the Raymond Loewy-designed Pennsylvania "Torpedo." An excellent article concerning Lionel's designs may be found in the Fall 1989 issue of *Classic Toy Trains*.

The largest version was an O Gauge 238, sold in either black or gun metal beginning in 1936. See color photo 16. It was a good seller and many have survived, but because of high demand by collectors, the prices tend to be high. By this date the company had renamed its Lionel Junior products, calling them simply "O27" to distinguish them from the higher-priced O Gauge trains. A wide range of Torpedos was also produced for O27 sets, including 2-4-2, 2-6-2 and clockwork models. The electric versions have automatic reversing, and some came with whistle tenders and automatic box couplers, so they are good candidates for operating use.

American Flyer's version of the Pennsy Torpedo was exclusively an economy model, and had a stamped sheet-metal body with minimal detailing and a simple box-shaped tender. Its first incarnation had a strange and highly unrealistic 0-4-2 wheel arrangement, later upgraded to a 2-4-4, and remote-control reversing was provided, although without a neutral position. These engines perform passably if not well, and mine has a wobble that has defied my best efforts at correction, but I like the way it looks at the head of a string of 6½-inch freight cars.

The products of each company tend to have a somewhat unified appearance, and I usually run them together when showing off the layout. Somehow a half-dozen American Flyer sets provide a more satisfying appearance than a mixture of Lionel and Flyer. Each firm's "style" seems to look best when kept in a homogeneous setting. This little Torpedo fits well in the company of large 3326 and 3308 steamers, providing a pleasant example of the "modern" approach to industrial design of the 1930s.

A personal favorite of mine in the streamlined steam category is Lionel's Commodore Vanderbilt, modeled after a New York Central prototype. Its gracefully shrouded body came in black, gun metal, red and blue, some with whistles and automatic couplers, and headed a variety of freight and passenger sets.

By the time of its introduction (1935) the company had developed a good working remote-control reverse unit and a smooth and powerful motor, and these little steamers make fine additions to an operating layout. Although the New York Central probably never ran a red engine, the Red Comet set pictured in color photo 17 was popular with buyers, and many can still be found, although often in poor condition.

A major weakness with the Commodore Vanderbilts was impurity of the alloy used in casting the cab. Usually the roof edges have been broken off, and other deterioration is frequently found. Fortunately, reproduction cabs and matching Lionel paint are easy to obtain.

This streamliner was also teamed up with the articulated cars from Flying Yankee sets (described below), with a special head-end car numbered "619" that is extremely hard to find today. There were two versions made: the Chrome Streak, with a black locomotive and two chrome-plated coaches; and the Blue Streak, a three-car set in medium blue from pilot to observation, featuring cars with white window stripes. See color photo 17.

Lionel built a beautiful model of the Milwaukee Road's Hiawatha locomotive from 1935 through 1942, with a long wheelbase that required O72 track with 6-foot-diameter circles. For the operator who, like myself, lacks the room for a layout of such large proportions, this locomotive is impractical for operation. (There is a limit to how far my wife will allow the trains to encroach upon the household, but the living room has space for those O72 curves; maybe someday . . .)

An attractive alternative exists, however. American Flyer also produced a fine-looking Hiawatha in 1936 and 1937, and sold it in both freight and passenger sets. The first version had a remote-control whistle and automatic reversing (a strange unit without a neutral position, described further in the discussion of Flyer's City of Denver set on next page). It needs 40-inch minimum diameter curves to operate well, thanks to a split pilot truck in which only the front axle pivots; some operators report a singular lack of success getting this model to track at all, but mine stays on the rails. The 1937 version had a fully turning four-wheel pilot truck and runs somewhat better, but lacks the whistle, which Flyer had moved to a trackside billboard that year.

In one set the locomotive came with a five-car string of long freight cars: gondola, crane, log car, tanker and caboose. Since the Milwaukee Hiawatha was a passenger locomotive, the prototype probably never saw freight service. Seeing a streamlined steamer hauling a crane is somewhat incongruous, but I like this set and run it frequently. The whistle unit originally required special four-railed track, so I've converted it to operate with a Lionel-type relay. I've also installed a modern E-unit for the advantage of a neutral position and dependability, so operating problems are rare. See color photo 8.

Diesel Streamliners

In prototype railroading, the beginning of the end for steam power appeared with the advent of the sleek streamlined passenger trains of the Burlington, Boston and Maine, Union Pacific and Illinois Central roads in the mid-1930s. Lionel and American Flyer (as well as Louis Marx, Hafner, and the lesser known firm of Hoge) quickly produced small-scale imitations, and they enjoyed wide distribution even during those Depression years. Most spectacular were Lionel's big O72 Union Pacific sets in yellow and brown or aluminum finishes, but these consists have been omitted from my layout because their long wheelbases require 6-foot curves.

Lionel produced streamliners in both O Gauge and O27, the latter still called "Lionel Junior" at that time. The Junior sets appeared in 1935, were sold for three years, and consisted of simple folded sheet metal locomotive and car units connected by rectangular vestibules suspended between them. The cars were unlighted and the windows unglazed, with small clockwork or electric motors used to power them. The electric versions are light in weight and run reasonably well, but their small size makes them look out of place with most other equipment.

The 1700 Lionel Junior in the photo below was originally red and chrome, but came to me badly rusted and dented, with a Marx motor installed in place of the original Lionel O27 unit. The motor was repairable, and I elected to paint the train in the same orange color that was used on the clockwork versions. Window glazing and interior lighting now enhance its appearance on the layout, and I run it mostly on the elevated portion toward the rear, where its small size contributes to the feeling of perspective (see Chapter Twelve).

This tiny streamlined diesel was Lionel's smallest in the 1930s, and provided remote-control reversing and a headlight in a very economical set. These units were not durably constructed, and many have failed to survive the years since production, but they look good, especially when run toward the back of a layout where their small size creates an illusion of distance.

Most common of the O Gauge sets were the Flying Yankees, patterned after the Boston and Maine articulated trains that served New England. They came either chrome plated or painted aluminum, with black, gray or red paint applied variously to nose and tail sections. All had remote-control reverse units, and many had whistles. The locomotive was economically made of sheet metal, and many were sold during the Depression years and have survived until today. The motor is easily serviced, as a single and easily removed screw drops it from the engine, and it performs well.

A die-cast engine body was used on the Union Pacific City of Denver model, painted in prototypical yellow and brown. The cars were the same as those used in Flying Yankee and Blue Streak sets, and were coupled to each other by means of a special vestibule. Except for the observation car, they had no wheels of their own. The vestibule unit rode on four wheels and

Boston & Maine's Flying Yankee diesels were good sellers for Lionel beginning in 1935, and are fine additions to an operating layout today. Full lighting and a powerful motor make them an attractive choice for passenger train fans. The version on the upper track is chrome plated with a gun metal cab, while the lower model is painted aluminum with a red cab roof. This latter set, available mostly through department stores, was uncatalogued.

had a circular spring-loaded plate inside that snapped over the cars' coupler bars when the button on top was pressed down.

This system was simple and effective, its only major fault being the tendency for the car ends to scratch the vestibule surfaces. Each connecting unit had a light bulb which illuminated the cars on either side. This design was a reasonably accurate representation of the prototype's articulated cars. The City of Denver set was introduced in 1936 with a whistle and a strong and reliable auto-reverse motor. See color photo 18.

American Flyer actually beat Lionel to the store shelves with the first streamliner for small-radius O Gauge curves in 1934, and by 1937 the firm's catalog featured four different locomotives of distinctive modern design. An artist's rendering on the inside front cover displayed them in attractive colors and larger-than-life perspective. Flyer's streamliners were designed for 40-inch-diameter curves, which allowed longer passenger cars than Lionel's 25 percent smaller O Gauge circles, and the company took advantage of this by creating long, sleek passenger sets. While not quite as impressive as the rival company's O72 streamliners, the Flyer models look both substantial and realistic without requiring unreasonable amounts of space for their trackwork.

The locomotives featured a variety of construction techniques. The Pennsylvania Torpedo was of stamped steel, and is described in the previous section of this chapter. The Hiawatha and City of Denver were die-castings, and the Burlington Zephyr was cast in aluminum and polished, rather than painted, to simulate the shiny exterior of the original. All but the Pennsy were offered with whistle units in 1936 only; the models pictured here are all 1936 production. The whistles were mounted in the first car behind the locomotive, and can be recognized by the three screws in the roof that hold the motor in place.

The American Flyer City of Denver was much more massive than Lionel's version; the locomotive measured nearly 13 inches and came with two foot-long coaches and an observation car nearly 2 inches longer. It had the same power unit as the Hiawatha, with large steamer-type wheels and a curious reverse unit built into the motor itself. The top of the motor's field was hinged at the front, held away from the armature by a spring, and had a metal lever projecting downward from the rear. When the field was energized by current passing through the motor, the hinged part of the field was magnetized and descended. The lever then moved a swiveling

AMERICAN FLYER MODEL TRAINS
More for your money in *Realism, Fun-Features and Performance*

The fascination of American Flyer Model Railroading never grows old. There's no greater fun in the world than running your own railroad, for you are the engineer at the throttle—the thrill is yours.

American Flyers are engineered from the same drawings and blue-prints that are used by the Railroads in producing their big trains. American Flyer models combine the maximum of scaled reproductions that permit their operating on a comparatively small 40" diameter circle of track. All of America's famous trains have been reproduced—they are models you will be proud to own.

AMERICAN FLYER MFG. CO., 2219-2239 South Halsted Street, Chicago, Illinois

Compare the giant six wheel drive Hudson Steam Type Locomotive and Train Sets shown on pages 12, 13, 14 and 15. This is typical of American Flyer values and clearly shows how much more you get for your money when you insist on American Flyer.

Let your Dad, Mother and Uncles in on your plans. Show them this catalog, and the illustration of the model you desire. They'll have as much fun running the train as you will. See these trains at your dealer. If he is unable to take care of your needs, ask him to order for you, or send a money order covering the cost direct to our Chicago Office, address shown below.

ALL TRAINS SHOWN IN THIS CATALOG HAVE THESE
Features

TRAIN SETS INCLUDE HIGH SPEED MODEL 40 INCH DIAMETER TRACK

HEAVY STEEL, FULL ENAMEL, BRASS TRIMMED CARS—NO LITHOGRAPH

ALL LOCOMOTIVES ARE EQUIPPED WITH REMOTE CONTROL MOTORS

BRASS TRIM, ENAMELED, FREIGHT CARS ARE THE LONGEST MADE

Pictured from left to right in both photos are the Pennsylvania Torpedo, U.P. City of Denver, Burlington Zephyr and Milwaukee Road Hiawatha, as shown in the 1937 American Flyer catalog and as they appear today in the author's collection.

set of contacts to one side or the other, causing the proper current flow for either reverse or forward motion.

My City of Denver had a complete reverse unit still intact, and I have been able to make it work with reasonable reliability. My Hiawatha, however, had lost the set of contacts at some time in the past.   Unlike Lionel's somewhat similar pendulum reverse of the late '20s, power was transmitted in the Flyer design through the motor's field and reverse lever directly to the contacts, making the substitution of a modern E-unit somewhat tricky. It can be done, however, by securing the hinged field permanently in place and rerouting the wiring. (If any reader wishes to undertake this conversion, I will be pleased to provide details.)

The car lights in the City of Denver shone through glazed windows, but there were no third-rail pickups on the two coaches, just on the observation car. Power for the bulbs was transmitted from both the locomotive and the observation car by means of spring contacts on the ends of the coaches. Each car had two trucks and could be used independently, and the ends were fitted with swiveling semi-vestibule sections that imitated the appearance of the articulated prototype. Few of these sets have survived in excellent condition today. They were constructed of riveted sheet metal, making disassembly for the purpose of restoration somewhat difficult, but the end results make the project worthwhile.

It is easy to understand why these units are often found in disfigured condition. The semi-vestibules fitted together with a tab and slot at the bottom, and the tops were secured by a thick wire brace that fit into a hole on the following car. It requires great care to insert this brace without marring the paint, and as young engineers are hardly noted for their patience, most Flyer streamliners have become chipped and scratched.

A remote-controlled whistle unit hung from the roof of the first passenger car, and was activated through a special Y-shaped pickup shoe on one truck. It required special four-rail track to operate (see Chapter Five for a photograph) and was discontinued after only one year, probably for reasons of economy. I have retained the whistle in my set, but added a Lionel DC relay to operate it, thus avoiding the need for special track.

The City of Denver was a handsome set, and moves in majestic fashion through my layout. It looks best on wide-radius curves, and I keep its speed down, not quite trusting the heavy locomotive casting to stay on the track. The motor is quiet and powerful, and the reverse unit rarely trips unexpectedly, thanks to a power feed from two pickups on the engine and through the lighting system from the observation car. It was pictured in the Flyer catalog for four years, and one or two examples seem to turn up at most large train meets. See color photo 19.

The most successful large streamliner to be produced by the Chicago-based firm was the cast-aluminum Burlington Zephyr. Built from 1934 through 1938, it came with two different power cars (narrow and wide) and two to four lighted cars, connected in the same manner as the Union Pacific set. A whistle was included only in the 1936 set pictured here, and the doors on the power unit and baggage car opened and closed. The castings were thick and surprisingly heavy for an aluminum toy. Performance is a bit sluggish, but it looks impressive when brightly polished (which is not a pleasant task!). The substantial construction has resulted in many survivors, and often the only restoration needed, other than rewiring, is a thorough cleaning and replacement of the decals.

The first version with a narrow cab did not have automatic reversing. The manual reverse lever was so completely concealed beneath the engine as to be almost useless. It is speculated that the wider body introduced in 1935 may have been necessitated by the inclusion of a larger motor with remote-controlled reverse. Whatever the reason, the larger Zephyr is much more impressive than the narrow 1934 model.

In addition to these premium-priced sets, American Flyer marketed numerous streamliners made of thin sheet steel, ranging from lightweight Zephyrs and Comets to tiny Minne-Ha-Ha and Hiawatha sets that were priced competitively with Lionel Juniors. Most were lithographed and flimsy in construction, lacking suitable reinforcement at the edges or internal bracing, and few have survived in good condition. They are very difficult to restore, with the exception of the enameled Illinois Central "Green Diamond" which was sold only in 1935.

As the first of the streamliners to be introduced by American Flyer, the shiny Burlington Zephyr model was cast from thick aluminum and came in three-, four- and five-unit sets.

This comparatively rare five-unit streamliner was finished in pea green with a tan stripe running its full length, and had both an Illinois Central and two square American Flyer Lines decals on each side. Each unit was open on one end; they connected to each other by means of a pin which fitted into a hole in the roof of the next car. The thin steel cars were easily dented, and because of their overall light weight combined with a heavy die-cast nose on the locomotive, this streamliner derails easily, making it subject to damage.

The cars were fully lighted, with window glazing and white simulated window shades. The motor ran quite fast on very low voltage, making it difficult to use on the same track with slower trains. There is another reason for leaving it on the shelf most of the time, however: it's ugly! (I admit to running it sometimes just to watch the effect it has on first-time visitors.)

Cataloged for only one year, the Illinois Central set by American Flyer, called the "Green Diamond" by collectors (although not by the manufacturer) after the prototype, was lightly constructed and more easily damaged than the heavier cast-bodied streamliners. Like the equally flimsy lithographed Zephyr and Comet sets by the same firm, it is rarely found today in good condition. It does display a certain style while slithering down the track, however, an image reinforced by its serpent-like snout. Flyer made many better looking trains!

This concludes the tour of some of my favorite pieces of motive power. Reviewing them in preparation for this book has reminded me once again of just how durable and well-made they are, and how they continue to please their owners so many years after first being sold. They squeak and groan occasionally to remind me to grease them a bit, but they seldom break down completely, and tolerate an amazing amount of neglect before needing attention. When repairs are needed, their tough and well-designed mechanisms respond to simple techniques and procedures, and almost any needed part can still be obtained today.

Collectors who wish to do their own repairs and restorations are encouraged to consult the excellent books on the subject which are available, including especially the aforementioned *Greenberg's Repair & Operating Manual: Prewar Lionel Trains*, written by John G. Hubbard. The same publisher also offers service manuals, parts lists and exploded diagrams to guide the inexperienced, and K-Line (P.O. Box 2831, Chapel Hill, North Carolina 27514) has reprinted many Lionel service and instruction sheets in book form. TM Books and Videos (P.O. Box 279, New Buffalo, Michigan 49117) also distributes repair instructions on video tape.

These publications provide step-by-step procedures for the servicing of motors, whistles, reverse units and accessories, with a heavy emphasis on Lionel. The principles involved are universal, and apply generally to Ives and American Flyer products as well, although a little supplementary guidance in the area of motor wiring might be in order here.

Locomotive Wiring Diagrams

A toy train motor is a relatively simple device, consisting of a magnetic field, an armature with commutator, and brushes. The field is wired to maintain a specific polarity, while the poles of the armature shift polarity according to which brush is in contact with the various segments of the commutator at any given time. As the current is directed to first one pole and then the next, a shifting pattern of magnetic attraction pulls the armature around in a circle, and this motion is transmitted to the drive wheels through a system of gears. In order for the motor to turn in the opposite direction, the ground and power leads are switched to reverse the pattern of magnetic attraction.

Most Lionel motors are wired in the same way, as illustrated in the various books and videos mentioned above. The method is diagramed here for reference. Note that the field is grounded, and the opposite end of the field coil is connected to one of the brushes through the reverse lever. The power lead from the third rail connects to the other motor brush as shown in the drawing. By moving the reverse lever to its alternate position, the power and ground leads to the brushes are reversed.

By contrast, the field in most American Flyer motors is connected directly to the power side (the third-rail pickup roller) and then to one of the brushes. The ground lead connects to the other brush directly. A confusing array of reverse mechanisms was produced by this firm, all of which accomplished the task of switching the ground and power leads to the brushes.

Most manual-reverse Ives locomotives have a complex pattern of wiring which reverses the flow of current through the field. This system is also diagramed. Some Lionel motors of the late 1930s and early '40s, such as those used in the most common O27 locos, also followed this pattern, with the automatic reverse mechanism (E-unit) wired directly to the field rather than the brushes.

Examination of these patterns should allow one to rewire most toy train motors, and to adapt them to the use of modern E-units if desired. Most other repairs described in the books and videos recommended here will work on all makes, needing only a little common sense on the modeler's part to account for the slight variations. However, everyone at some time will likely face a problem beyond his or her expertise, and that is when membership in one or more of the collectors' associations proves its worth. It has been my experience that people involved in this hobby are more than willing to share their knowledge, usually for no more than the cost of a phone call.

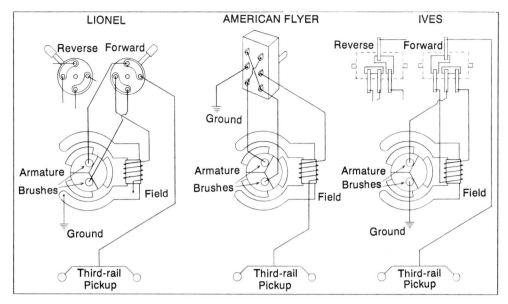

Although the principles of electric motor operation remain the same, the various manufacturers routed the wiring in their locomotives in slightly different ways. These diagrams illustrate the fundamental differences between the methods employed by Lionel, American Flyer and Ives, including manual reverse levers. Ground wires are interconnected through the motor frame to the wheels, and thus to the ground rail of the track. Both forward and reverse positions are shown for Lionel and Ives, the former with a disk-type switch and the latter with a revolving drum. Should one of these reverse levers be damaged or missing, it can easily be replaced by a double-pole, double-throw toggle switch, as shown wired to the American Flyer motor. For hints on repairing Lionel's auto-reverse E-unit, see John Hubbard's **Greenberg's Repair And Operating Manual: Prewar Lionel Trains.**

Light Up Your Locomotives!

Before moving on to the topic of rolling stock, I would like to recommend a minor modification that greatly increases the appeal of toy locomotives when they are running on a layout: lights! Even those collectors who are reluctant to alter their units in any way can place a bulb or two in the cab of an electric-outline loco or Hiawatha without diminishing the engine's value in any way.

The easiest method uses bayonet-based bulbs and sockets. A stiff wire of appropriate length is soldered to the outside terminal on the socket. A lug is crimped on the other end of the wire, and is grounded to the chassis by placing it under any convenient motor-mounting screw. The other terminal is wired to the power pickup (usually the locomotive headlight wire is the easiest to connect to) and the task is complete. The miniature engine crew can now see to run the train.

The effect of these lights is enhanced by glazing the windows with clear or frosted celluloid, held in place by Scotch Magic transparent tape, which adheres tightly to metal but leaves no residue when removed. Color photo 20 shows the difference between a factory original and a lighted cab.

Another easy modification imitates a feature found on the biggest steamers from both major manufacturers of the '30s: the firebox light. This glow from beneath the cab of a Flyer 3326 or Lionel 260E can be reproduced in virtually any locomotive that has a little bit of room above the trailing truck, by using a socket and red-tinted bulb wired in the same manner as the box cab lights described above. If space is at a premium, a sub-miniature screw-based bulb and socket can be fitted in almost anywhere. The effect of such illuminating additions in a darkened layout room is magic!

Now that the power units are lined up and ready to go, we have to have some cars for them to pull.

EIGHT

Rolling Stock

For purposes of explanation, representative samples of the freight and passenger cars sold by Lionel, Ives and American Flyer are pictured in this chapter, but no attempt has been made to list them in their entirety. Readers may view most of them in the various Greenberg *Guides* for each manufacturer, the Train Collectors Association publication *Lionel Trains, Standard of the World, 1900-1943* and the Tuohy and McComas series on Lionel.

Choosing rolling stock for an operating layout is a matter of both taste and function. Aesthetic considerations and operating potential have governed which items I enjoy running the most, and such opinions differ widely among collectors. In general, all of these items are trouble-free, and most are readily available in all levels of condition, from Poor to Like New. Restorable examples are usually reasonably priced (except for the rarest) and provide many hours of enjoyment for those who delight as I do in making old wrecks look factory fresh. As in the case of locomotives, enameled cars lend themselves to restoration much more easily than do the lithographed ones.

Freight Cars Came in Two Sizes!

Each of the major manufacturers of toy trains in America produced two distinct lines of freight cars in the Prewar years, large and small. Accuracy of scale was not a major consideration until the late 1930s, and size was equated with price, quality and features. The small series of cars came with smaller locomotives in low-priced sets, while their bigger counterparts accompanied more expensive motive power and had a greater number of features and details.

It is interesting to note that the early O Gauge cars made by different manufacturers may be mixed together, especially the small ones, as they are comparable in size and configuration and have mostly compatible couplers. The photo illustrates freight cars from four different manufacturers.

Early Lionel O Gauge freight cars are divided into the little 800-series with four wheels and the eight-wheeled 820s. Each series contained a boxcar, stock car and caboose, and there was also a four-wheeled gondola numbered 901 that matched the 800s in size.

Beginning about 1923, the company revised and increased the overall sizes of both lines, but retained the same approximate numbering system. The 800s grew to about 6½ inches, and eventually contained eight types of cars: hopper, gondola, tank car, stock car, boxcar, flatcar

Thanks to their hook couplers, these cars can be used together in the same train, although made by four different companies: Lionel, Ives, American Flyer and Dorfan. They are close in size and not too unlike in style, thus presenting a pleasing appearance when mixed together.

with lumber, dump car and caboose. All had four wheels, and continued to be offered right up until World War II, although they were deleted from the catalog with the advent of the 650 series, built to the same dimensions but with eight wheels.

The larger freights now began with the number "810" (which was assigned to the crane), and were highly detailed heavyweight cars. These were entirely new cars built on frames that were nearly 9 inches long and came in nine types: boxcar, gondola, stock car, crane, tanker, lumber car, hopper, searchlight car and caboose. They were trimmed with brass plates, handrails and brakewheels (features that were also added later to the small cars), and came in a great variety of colors.

In the mid-'20s Lionel introduced a new latch-type coupler for both cars and locomotives. For a brief transitional period, these couplers had slots to allow them to mate with older hook-equipped cars; these are usually referred to as "combination" couplers. The slots were removed by 1928, which meant that buyers could no longer connect their old and new cars.

Beginning in 1915, Lionel produced two sizes of freight cars in two price ranges, distinguished mainly by cost and number of wheels. The smallest boxcar (less than 6 inches long) was numbered "800", and the 7¼-inch one was "820".

This Lionel 252 built in 1924 has a combination latch with a slot to accommodate older cars with hook couplers. The 529-series passenger cars that came with it had latches without slots.

Lionel packaged the small freight cars with such locomotives as the 248 and 252 box cabs, while the big 254 St. Paul and 251 New York Central-style electrics pulled the larger ones. The mid-sized 253 New Haven box cab looks good with either size.

All of Lionel's freight cars from this period were well built from heavy gauge steel. While some of their trim may be fragile (such as the stanchions that support the handrails on tank cars), restoration is relatively easy and replacement parts are plentiful.

Although built to the same gauge, these Lionel 803 and 816 hopper cars seem to belong to different scales. While their latch-type couplers are compatible, they do not look good together in the same train, and should be matched with comparably sized locomotives.

Most Ives freight cars had lithographed sides and came in sizes which were comparable to Lionel's. They were first equipped with hook couplers and later with an automatic design that retained a slot to allow connection with the older hooks. The tiniest were 4½ inches long (50 series) and rode on four wheels. The next larger had either four (560 series) or eight (60 series) wheels, and were about the same size as Lionel 800s, an average of 5½ inches long.

Seven body types were offered: caboose, gondola (cataloged as a gravel car), stock car, merchandise (box) car, lumber car, refrigerator and tanker. The large Ives freights (120 series) were in the 9-inch range and had two four-wheel trucks. These were produced in the same styles as the smaller cars, minus the tanker.

These products were made from thin, lightweight steel, and have not survived as well as the Lionel cars. Their truss rods are easily bent or broken, and the fragile cross bars of the stock cars are readily distorted by routine handling, especially by children. Examples in excellent condition command high prices, and since most are lithographed, they are difficult to restore.

When Ives was taken over by Lionel and American Flyer in 1928, and by Lionel exclusively a year later, several cars were produced with a mixture of parts from all three companies, such as an Ives-framed 122 tank car with the body from a Lionel 815. Lionel also introduced newly designed gondola, box, stock and caboose models in a 10-inch length, equipped with Lionel latch couplers but bearing the Ives name. These were later renamed with Lionel identification and sold in uncataloged sets after the Ives trademark was allowed to disappear.

Another group of lithographed freight cars was produced by Lionel for its Ives line, the same approximate size as the 800 series. They had eight wheels but relatively simple construction, and were intended for low-priced sets. After the Ives line was discontinued, these cars were developed into the O27 line and continued until World War II, eventually receiving automatic couplers and more highly detailed bodies. All examples, including those with Ives nameplates, had Lionel-style latch or box couplers.

Roughly equivalent to Lionel products in size, these Ives 65 (small) and 127 (large) stock cars had lithographed sides and relatively fragile construction.

American Flyer's O Gauge line was similarly divided into two basic size ranges. The smallest were 5½

Originally produced for the subsidiary Ives nameplate in 1932, these large but economical lithographed freight cars were marketed by Lionel in uncatalogued sets during the 1930s.

to 6½ inches, and had four- or eight-wheeled frames. Sides on the earlier examples were lithographed, while enameled cars replaced them beginning about 1930. They were offered with hook couplers throughout their life span, right up until the war years.

There were eight different cars available: caboose, boxcar, gondola (called a "sand" car in the catalogs), log car, stock car, dump car, crane (rare) and tanker. In addition, the company made two series of very light, low-priced lithographed cars during the Depression: the tiny "Hummer" line and a slightly larger group that was sold in sets with such locomotives as the inexpensive sheet metal Hiawatha.

Large Flyer freights measured 9½ inches in length, and while the early lithographed models are quite rare, enameled versions are common and easily acquired for low prices at train meets. They came in nine distinct designs: box, log, tank, gondola ("sand" car), crane, dump, milk, floodlight and caboose, plus a "machinery" car that was identical to the log car but lacked its wooden load.

These large cars suffered from the company's indecision over coupler design in the 1930s. They may be found with incompatible hooks, curly-Q knuckles and automatic latches, depending upon year of manufacture. Otherwise they changed very little, although the 1939 and later models with automatic couplers ride closer to the rails.

These cars were substantially built, and look especially good behind Flyer's large steamers, such as the 3326 model. They are longer in relation to their girth than Lionel's large cars, and look more like the prototype, although the huge brakewheels seem very much out of place. See color photo 21.

This Ives 1680 tank car was a Lionel product of 1931 and '32, and was not compatible with earlier Ives equipment because of its latch couplers. Lionel converted these low-priced items into the O27 line, including this 2680 Shell model, and continued them until the Second World War forced an end to production.

*American Flyer's small lithographed freight cars such as this 1118 tanker and 1114
caboose are relatively easy to find, as are the later enameled series. Among the latter, the
3012 boxcar is common, but the 3009 dump car was made for only two years, and is scarce.*

After the Gilbert acquisition in 1938, the company emphasized its new line of 3/16-inch scale
trains, and developed a variety of die-cast and sheet metal freight cars. Many can be found at
low prices today for the operator who favors this size.

The offerings of the Lionel Corporation deserve further attention, as a new series of cars was
introduced in 1933, the 650 type. The bodies were adapted from the small 800-series cars,
mounted on a frame with two four-wheel trucks. Latch couplers were installed on the earlier
cars, then manual box couplers beginning in 1936. Cars equipped with automatic box couplers
had the prefix "2" added to their catalog numbers beginning in 1938; for example, the 657 caboose
had manual couplers, and the 2657 had automatic ones.

Over the years some changes were made in trim and decoration: brass plates gave way to
nickel and finally to rubber-stamped lettering and decals; bright journals were replaced with
black; colors changed; and the frames were altered to accept new truck and coupler designs.
New cars were added that had not been included in the 800 series, such as the 620 floodlight and
2660 crane. Ten types were made overall: hopper, flat (lumber), floodlight, gondola, stock, box,
tank, dump, crane and caboose. See color photo 22.

The large cars underwent similar changes; colors of paint were altered, couplers changed,
and rubber-stamped lettering replaced the brass and nickel plates, but the basic bodies remained
the same, and except for the operating cars described below, nothing new was created.

Some old favorites were refurbished to give them a fresh appearance, and presumably more
sales appeal. The huge 810 crane, for example, had for years been painted terra cotta, with a
maroon roof and peacock blue boom, a bit bright perhaps, but less gaudy than the red and yellow
version that replaced it in 1935. See color photo 23.

Similarly, the floodlight car went from terra cotta to green, the tanker from green to
aluminum or orange, and the caboose from peacock and green to all red. Most of the cars were
redecorated at least twice, and the final rubber-stamped examples were handsome and more
subdued in color, but did not sell in large numbers and are scarce today.

There are probably several reasons for their relative lack of popularity. The smaller 650
series, equipped with pairs of four-wheel trucks and additional trim, and expanded to include
a crane and searchlight, were both attractive and easier for young children to handle. For the
opposite end of the market (the older and more serious model railroader), Lionel had introduced
its new line of scale and semi-scale freight cars. The overweight and somewhat foreshortened
810-series cars seemed old-fashioned by comparison. (The scale and scale-detailed cars were a
foretaste of Lionel's more realistic look after the war. I do not mix them with my "toy" types,
but some operators may wish to.)

Lionel's new automatic couplers brought with them an important new feature, the means
for providing auxiliary power on demand through the sliding pickup shoes mounted underneath. These shoes received current from the two extra rails on the uncoupling ramp at the touch
of a button (see Chapter Five), and were grounded through the cars' wheels. By rerouting the

Contributing to the popularity of Lionel's small line of O Gauge freight cars, the 2620 floodlight and 2660 crane gave children more to do with their toys, and saved Father the price differential charged for the larger series equivalents.

current so that one shoe was a ground, a circuit could also be provided to operate a solenoid, again at the operator's command.

A solenoid is simply a coil of wire that creates a magnetic field, causing a rod in the center of that field to move. It is a fairly powerful device, and Lionel used it to raise the coupler boxes and to tilt the beds of dump cars to make them unload.

Operating cars were made in both small and large versions, three each in the 650 and 810 series. The lumber cars (both large and small) had four stakes, two of which collapsed outward when the opposite side of the bed tilted upward to dump the logs. The red and black dump cars (again in two sizes) had swiveling trays that poured coal into a trackside bin or the 97 coal loader (see Chapter Ten).

Two fascinating cars were each made in one size only. The small 3652 gondola had a hinged side instead of a tilting bed; in fact, the bottom of the car was built on a slant, which kept its load of barrels leaning against the movable side. When its solenoid was energized, the side tilted outward and the barrels cascaded out at trackside.

Most complicated of all was the big 3814 merchandise car. Outwardly similar to the 2814 boxcar, it was fitted with a ramp-like mechanism with a moving bar that pushed small packing crates one by one to an ejection plate at the door. Each touch of the control button tossed a crate out and advanced the next one into position. After every five deliveries, the door closed by itself. Crates could be reloaded through a hatch in the roof.

First introduced in 1938, the big 3859 dump car and its smaller 3659 cousin were the first of Lionel's remote-control unloading freight cars. The 3652 barrel-dumping gondola and 3651 lumber car followed in 1939, adding a new dimension to toy train fun.

The automatic cars all had remote-control couplers, and carried the prefix "3" instead of "2" in their catalog numbers. They were made in substantial quantities, especially the smaller versions. For any layout that features Lionel's four magnificent Prewar operating accessories (see Chapter Ten), they are essential.

Passenger Cars Came in Many Sizes!

Unlike items of freight, passengers were carried in cars with widely varying dimensions on Prewar toy train layouts. Lionel built them to match every size of locomotive manufactured.

The earliest were tiny 600s and mid-sized 601s and 610s, the former well suited to such locomotives as the 150 with a 5-inch cab, and the latter looking correct with engines 154 and 156 (with 8½- and 10-inch frames respectively). These sizes were first built in 1915. An observation car (612) was built to match the 8½-inch 610 model, and the 7-inch 601 had a matching 602 baggage car and a companion coach numbered 603.

Both of these Lionel coaches were designed to run on O Gauge track, but other than for humorous effect, they are not meant to coexist on the layout. No other company made so wide a range of sizes in a single gauge.

These were later joined by an in-between size, the 6½-inch-long model of slightly more modern design that shared the 603 numbering. This design had five window openings, compared with the earlier 603's seven, but each was divided into two panes and a transom by a metal insert panel, a feature first included in the 610s and 612s. These and the 610 series were the first to have interior lights in O Gauge, beginning in 1923.

Unlike its two major competitors, the Lionel Corporation made no lithographed passenger cars, except for the clockwork and Winner cars and the very inexpensive 1690 types that were included in O27 sets in the 1930s. The others were finished in enamel, and in all but the early 600s, contrast was provided by the insert panels that outlined the windows and provided doors and number boards. This design feature also strengthened the cars by giving them double sides, and made assembly (not to mention restoration!) easy.

All but the least expensive were lighted by means of pickup rollers on the trucks. Starting in 1924, five new models replaced the earlier ones, built in differing sizes to match the various box cab locomotives of the period. Beginning with the smallest, they were numbered

Lionel's first lighted O Gauge passenger cars appeared in 1923, rode on eight-wheeled trucks and came first with hook couplers and later with latches. They matched the size of the larger 154 box cab locomotive.

"529-530" and "629-630" for the 6½-inch size; "603", "604", "607", "608", "609" and "611" (7½ inches); "610" and "612" (8¾ inches); "605" and "606" (10¼ inches); and 11½-inch giants numbered "710" and "712".

These cars survived only until the early 1930s, when they were gradually replaced by new lower-profile designs (except for the 603 types, which were included especially in uncataloged sets through 1942.) They are bulky, well made and brightly painted in a wide variety of colors, and convey a mixed impression of both toys and authentic railroading atmosphere. Most convincing are the 605s and 710s, which have a more realistic window size and arrangement and prototypical clerestory roofs.

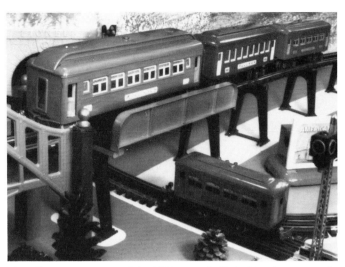

Lionel's passenger cars of the 1920s were built in five sizes to match the firm's various locomotives, and came in many different color combinations. Beginning with the largest, the four pictured here are 710-, 610-, 607- and 529-series designs.

One of the earliest of the company's more realistic passenger designs was created for the Ives division in 1932, and ranks high among my favorites. Although sparsely trimmed (they lacked steps on the ends, for example), their foot-long measurements and low roof line make them very attractive on the rails. Baggage, coach and observation models were made in several different colors, and while those carrying Ives stamping are rare, the later Lionel-labeled versions were included in quite a few uncataloged sets and can still be readily found today. (Unfortunately for the buyer, the prices are high, as they are in great demand by collectors because of their handsome appearance.)

These 1685-series cars, originally designed by Lionel for the Ives line in 1932, were available in uncataloged sets through 1937, and in the opinion of the author are the best-looking coaches the company ever made.

I team them up with my gun metal gray 249 steamer, and with a customized silver 262 (shown in color photo 14). Operators who favor the later scale-detailed locomotives (224, 225, 226 and 229, for example) will also find them a good choice.

Most of these models had four-wheel trucks, although the scarce gray and maroon versions with six-wheelers are particularly good looking. Other available color combinations include three different shades of red with maroon roofs and the blue and silver scheme shown here. The roofs had clever spring-loaded clips that allowed easy access to the light bulbs inside.

This roof design was also used on two premium series which were introduced in 1931 and 1933 respectively: the 613/614/615 and 600/601/602 groups, each containing baggage, coach and observation cars. Although shorter (at 10¼ and 9 inches) than the 1685s, they are nevertheless attractive, and very well built. Both types were renumbered with a "2" prefix when equipped with automatic couplers, and remained in the catalog through 1942. See color photo 24.

A similar group of cars, slightly undersized but with even better proportions, came with lower-priced sets from 1938 until the war. Their simpler construction (roofs held by a knurled bolt instead of spring clips, and lack of such trim as handrails) kept costs down, but they are still handsome and go well with smaller locomotives such as the O27 Torpedos. They number in the 1630s and 1640s (or 2630 and 2640 for the auto-coupler versions), and are found in blue, green and brown.

All of Lionel's passenger cars described here are excellent candidates for a display layout. Most are lighted, well built and colorful, and worn examples make fine restoration projects. Dry transfer lettering is readily available to return them to their original appearance.

The company also made very long streamlined cars to go with the Union Pacific diesels, scale Hudsons and Hiawathas (the "Rail Chief" style), plus a nicely scaled plastic heavyweight Pullman usually referred to as an "Irvington" or "Madison" car. I don't use either of these types; the former require 6-foot-diameter curves, and the latter are more closely associated with the more realistic styles of the Postwar period.

The rival firms of Ives and American Flyer used the lithograph process to create a wide range of attractive passenger cars through the mid-'20s. The first and smallest Ives examples (50 series) measured just 4 inches over their four-wheeled frames, but grew to 5¼ inches in 1910. The 60 series, both four- and eight-wheeled versions, were first 6 inches, then 6⅜ inches in length. Two of these cars are pictured with the clockwork set in Chapter Seven.

The earliest 70-series cars were considerably larger at 11⅝ inches in length, having been adapted from the former No. 1 Gauge production. These were available for only two years, 1912 and 1913. The 70-series designation was revived in 1923 to renumber the old 60-series cars (still measuring about 6⅜ inches), and the same frame sometimes carried bodies numbered "550", "551" and "552".

Larger lithographed cars were numbered "129" to "132", and were made in four types (baggage, combination, coach and observation) and a variety of highly detailed color schemes. They measured 9 to 9½ inches long, were sold from 1904 to 1930, and were often lighted by pickup rollers on the trucks. Early versions had plain trucks, but brass journals were added about 1926. Color photo 25 shows both types.

Like all cars with printed rather than enameled sides, these Ives products are hard to restore, and are somewhat fragile. Their light weight sometimes causes tracking problems, since in strings of more than four, the lead cars are often pulled off the track on sharp curves. Their fine appearance makes enduring these problems worthwhile, however, and they provide a nice contrast to the more familiar Lionel outlines.

Largest and best proportioned of the lithographed cars produced by American Flyer, the Illini series was catalogued from 1922 through 1927, and available for several years thereafter. Examples in good condition command high prices, but they are a handsome addition to any layout, especially behind the impressive 3020 box cab loco. It is hard to make up matched sets from individual cars, as the shades of green on the lithographed sides ranged from medium to dark.

American Flyer also produced tiny, medium and large cars by the lithograph process. The earliest (called "Chicago" cars after the stamping on the side) were only 4½ inches long and rode on four wheels; a slightly longer and very scarce version came with eight. More common were the 1107, 1108 and 1120 cars of the 'teens and '20s, lettered in a variety of road names and built on 5½-inch four-wheeled frames as late as 1934.

Among the rarest are the "Dominion Flyer" cars produced for the Canadian market, and sold largely by mail order through such firms as the T. Eaton Company (the north-of-the-border equivalent to Sears and Roebuck in the United States). Found in both Canadian National and Canadian Pacific versions, these scarce cars are usually scratched or damaged, in part because of their lightweight construction. The examples shown in color photo 26 were produced in 1924, and purchased in their original box at an auction in Nova Scotia (see Chapter One).

Slightly larger at 6½ inches, various 1100- and 1200-series cars came in both four- and eight-wheel configurations and a variety of colors. Some bore no numbers, but had names such as "Paul Revere" and "Lexington" printed on the sides. Largest of all, prior to the introduction of enameled cars, was the 9½-inch group of Columbia and Illini coaches in varying shades of green and brown. They were first cataloged in 1922, and came either with hook couplers or the special harpoon design when packed with the 3020 box cab electric.

The earliest examples were lighted by means of external wiring that plugged into a hole just below the lip of the roof at the end, connecting to a similar receptacle on the locomotive body; later versions had individual pickup rollers on the trucks. Sliding baggage car doors added greatly to play value for children, and changing the bulbs was easy, thanks to removable roofs. These well-proportioned cars look fine on a layout and are in great demand, especially in matched sets, since the colors varied widely.

Probably because of competition from Lionel, both Ives and Flyer switched to enameled cars with brass plates in the latter part of the 1920s. Although neither as detailed nor as realistic as the lithographed models, they were attractive to buyers and were produced in various sizes. Ives made them in 8- and 10-inch sizes during their last few years of production before and during the Lionel takeover, and American Flyer made 6½-, 8¼-, 9½- and 11-inch lengths. See color photo 27.

The Flyer cars were available throughout the 1930s, and had either brass trim or simulated brass decals, as shown in the photo below. Even some of the cheapest versions were lighted, using an interesting third-rail pickup arm. The roller was suspended from a flexible brass strip, which in turn was fastened directly to the internal light socket through an insulating bushing. This low-cost arrangement required fewer man-hours to install than conventional separate sockets with their associated wiring.

The large cars, by contrast, were highly labor intensive. Unlike their Lionel counterparts, in which a single metal insert provided all the window frames and number boards for each car side, Flyer cars had a separate window frame surrounding each opening. As many as twenty-eight pieces of trim were applied to the largest coaches, counting the name and number plates. These parts fall off frequently, and are easily lost.

These low-priced 6½-inch cars by American Flyer were lighted by a single bulb in a socket mounted directly on the floor. A brass strip attached to the underside of the socket suspended the roller over one axle, where it contacted the third rail. The window trim is made from brass, but the nameplates and doors are decals.

This presents a special problem for restorers; I have yet to find anyone making reproductions of these window frames, and had to fashion my own for a set of "Potomac" cars that came with my 3116 St. Paul electric. The same problem exists with Ives cars, which also had individual window frames.

Any of these Ives and Flyer cars work well on a display layout; the choice depends upon availability and the operator's taste. In general, the smaller cars are easy to find in almost any condition, from poor to like new, and except as noted above they are easy to recondition.

When A. C. Gilbert acquired control of the firm, American Flyer began producing die-cast and sheet metal cars in ³/₁₆-inch scale to match the new line of smaller and more realistic locomotives. Some were continued in S Gauge after the war. They do not fit in well with regular O Gauge equipment, unless run at the back to increase the illusion of distance.

Restoration Techniques

John G. Hubbard's *Greenberg's Repair & Operating Manual: Prewar Lionel Trains* contains some excellent suggestions for restoration, repair of sheet metal and cast parts, and touch-up painting; I recommend it highly. The beginner would be wise to follow his hints, and should practice on low-value items until the necessary skills are acquired.

The following procedures are not directed toward those who seek a museum-quality restoration, but wish instead to produce fine-looking models with a factory-fresh appearance for a display layout. The newness will mellow with time, or you can follow Mr. Hubbard's ideas about simulating a patina of age.

One should remember that the value of many toy trains lies in the rarity of the finish, and such examples should not be stripped and repainted. The extremely rare Ives Standard Gauge No. 3243 locomotive in white, for example, differs from the green or orange examples in no way other than color. Refinishing it would reduce its value to the lowest common denominator, no matter what color is chosen.

Therefore the best candidates for refinishing are those badly marred items, the value of which is in the structure rather than the decoration. Lionel made thousands upon thousands of 657 cabooses in several different color schemes, with almost none of them considered to be scarce (although one should learn the details of the two known rarities, just in case). Stripping and repainting any of these for layout use is certainly justifiable, unless one is content to run shabby, dented equipment.

Should old toy trains ever be painted in color schemes that did not originate at the factory? I think so, as long as only relatively common pieces are handled in this manner. One hardly restores an 831 lumber car intending to make a fortune from its resale, but rather for the personal satisfaction of using it to enhance the layout. If I choose to paint it bright orange instead of its original dark green, and the results please me from an aesthetic point of view, I consider it acceptable.

If a locomotive or car reaches me in poor condition, I believe it to be fair game for customizing, unless a particular color combination is required by its configuration. I would not have repainted my American Flyer Hiawatha in any but the original orange, gray and black; but a generic Lionel 262, which represents no specific prototype, can be redone in silver as an eye-catcher without offending too many people (I hope!).

Spreading the side frames of the trucks slightly will allow the wheels and axles to fall out for cleaning. The journal boxes are fastened in with tabs, one of which must be straightened for removal; it should be bent gradually, and no more than absolutely necessary.

Now, how do we do it? The supplies needed are minimal: paint stripper, rust remover, metal polish, spray paint, a few basic tools and lots of patience.

The first step is to disassemble the car or locomotive. I have chosen a beat-up Lionel 603 from a Red Comet set to use as an example. The wheels are removed by spreading the truck side frames just enough to allow the axles to drop out. The journals are removed by bending one of the metal tabs slowly and carefully, just enough to free it from the truck. I soak all of these parts in rust remover if there is any trace of corrosion, then wash them in a strong cleaner and dry them with a hair dryer to keep rust from forming again.

A very light polishing of the wheels and axles with a cloth impregnated with thin oil is the final step toward preservation. Only the slightest trace of oil should be used, as it contaminates the trackwork when the cars are run. The journal boxes (and other shiny parts such as handrails from cars so equipped) can be treated with metal polish for a like-new shine. The work is tedious but worth the effort.

The roof is held on by a single central bolt, and removing it allows access to the other parts. The couplers are fastened by twist tabs, which can be straightened with pliers (slowly and gradually to prevent undue weakening at the bend) until they drop out of the holes in the floor. The trucks are held in place by small lock washers, and will release if the washers are pried up gently on the thinner side. On some cars, horseshoe-shaped fasteners are used instead; these can be removed by spreading their ends slightly with the blade of a screwdriver.

Lionel trucks were manufactured from painted or blackened metal. In either case, after I have removed any accumulated rust, I spray them flat black and bake the finish for twenty minutes in a home-built oven made from a wooden milk crate and two 100-watt light bulbs. (Don't use the oven in the kitchen unless you love the smell of baked paint; it takes days for it to dissipate.) More about painting will follow.

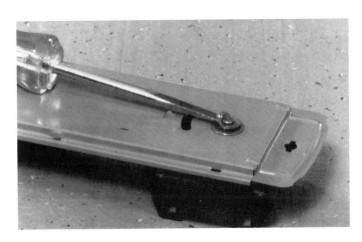

The lock washer that holds a Lionel truck in place can be removed by inserting a small screwdriver under the raised portion and bending up carefully until it releases. The process is reversed for reassembly. This washer fits in a groove encircling the portion of the truck that protrudes through the hole in the car floor.

Tabs holding the other parts of the car together should be bent back carefully just enough to allow them to slip out of their slots. If one breaks off, a substitute can be cut from brass stock and soldered in place; it's an exacting job requiring patience and practice, but it can be done so it will be invisible from outside the car. (Alternatively, the parts can be reassembled later with epoxy, although I do not favor this method. I have successfully repaired cars that have been disassembled at least twice before and lost all their original tabs, without having to resort to glue.)

Tabs can often be preserved by twisting them after reassembly, rather than bending them over. They are weakened most by repeated bending at the same joint, and twisting them instead to keep them in the slots puts the stress at a different location.

After all parts have been separated, the paint can be removed. Any bent or dented parts may be straightened first, or after the old finish has been stripped.

This should be done outdoors if possible, or otherwise under very well-ventilated conditions. A respirator-type face mask and rubber gloves are recommended, as the fumes from the paint

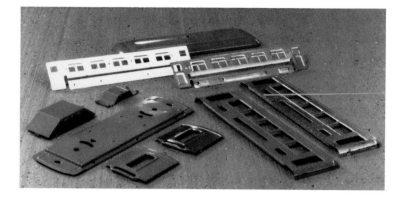

Removal of the old paint exposes the tinplate surface of the car parts. It must be cleaned thoroughly before repainting to ensure a sound new coat. The finish should be baked and then left for a day or two to harden before handling.

remover cannot tell skin and lung tissue from enamel, and will damage both! Once the chemical has soaked in (anywhere from a few seconds to ten minutes, depending upon the kind of paint), I use a stiff brush to remove it, wash off the residue with a hose, and finish up with a strong cleaner. Thorough rinsing of the cleaning agent is necessary, or any new paint will not adhere.

Once any needed repairs are completed, the next step is the building of supports from scrap wood to hold the various parts for painting. A good primer coat is essential, sprayed on lightly and evenly (outdoors again, if possible; the fumes are persistent, and I do all restoration during the warm months to avoid contaminating the house or my family's respiratory systems). Twenty minutes in the oven and a brief cooling-off period is required between coats.

The final color is best applied in two coats, sprayed lightly to avoid runs in a dust- and wind-free atmosphere. Since I paint outdoors, I have built a windbreak to ensure this. Next the parts should be baked and left to harden for a day or two before being handled. (I use spray paint made by Mr. Charles Wood of Classic Model Trains, Hartford, Ohio 44424. The color fidelity, durability and smoothness of finish are, in my opinion, superior.)

A word of caution is in order. Aerosol paint will deposit itself on surfaces a surprising distance from the work place. Baffles should be set up to protect any objects in the surrounding area. Recent concerns over the environment have also caused me to begin to reconsider my use of these products in outdoor locations. I am currently seeking to borrow time in a facility capable of treating the air prior to exhausting it into the atmosphere (such as an auto paint shop) where I might do my spraying.

Reassembly is just a reversal of the take-apart process. For the inexperienced, I recommend taking notes and labeling parts as they come off, especially in the case of locomotives with several different sizes of screws. The pictures in the Greenberg *Guides* serve as good reference material if the location of a part is forgotten. In general, toy train construction is such that most parts will only fit one way.

The last step is replacement of lettering by decal or dry transfer. This car was done with Bennett Dry Transfers (P.O. Box 178, Closter, New Jersey 07624), a

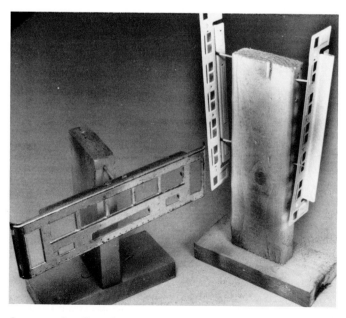

Scrap wood, nails and wire can be used to make temporary supports for parts to be painted. They allow the object to be turned in any required direction to ensure complete spray coverage.

source licensed by Lionel to produce reproductions for almost every conceivable Lionel, Ives or Flyer product. In my experience, the quality of these transfers has been first rate. Instructions for easy application are printed in Janice Bennett's catalog. See color photo 28.

Lights Bring a Layout to Life!

Foremost among the powerful memories of my childhood that frequently surface at unexpected moments in my life is the vivid recollection of running my Lionel tracks under my bed, dresser and chest of drawers, then turning out the room lights and watching the headlight of the locomotive trace patterns as it passed in and out amid the furniture. In my mind were created mountain passes, urban canyons and tunnels of every possible description, night scenes brightened by the progress of my own iron horse.

Today I flood my layout with lights of every kind. Floodlamps brighten the train yards, houses glow with warmth, and businesses and industries shine with activity. Lamp posts guide pedestrians through my towns, and most importantly, my trains sparkle and gleam from every possible window.

The locomotive cabs shine, fireboxes glow red, and the crews gather around lanterns in cabooses and baggage cars. From the observation platforms, red marker lights mark the passage of coaches vanishing into tunnels, and brilliant headlights herald the emergence of powerful streamliners coming down from the hills.

Those fine folks at Lionel, Ives and American Flyer helped me along before the war with quite a few miniature bulbs, but where they fell short, I take up the slack. Let's begin with the little 603 Red Comet coach that we have just restored.

This design was Lionel's longest-running passenger car style, and in most incarnations it had interior lights. Why the beautiful Red Comet should have remained dark is a mystery to me, but

The cross brace on the truck from this 603 coach is easily replaced with a commercially made pickup roller and bracket made especially for this purpose and sold by most toy train parts suppliers.

A single miniature bolt attaches the light socket to the upper cross brace inside this Lionel No. 603 coach, just as it does in the factory-lighted 607 cars of the same design. The flex wire is passed through a hole in the floor, to be attached to the terminal on the pickup roller. That's all there is to it!

the situation can easily be remedied. All that is needed can be purchased from any parts supplier: a pickup roller and bracket, a socket with a fiber insert, a bulb, and some flexible wire.

A cross brace is removed from one truck and replaced by the pickup assembly. Since most cars of this type were lighted, the trucks were built for this purpose, and a standard replacement part fits easily. Next a piece of flex wire is soldered to the center contact on the fiber insert and placed inside the socket, which is then bolted in place on the roof-support bracket; the hole for this was factory-installed! The other end of the wire is fed through the hole in the floor provided for just this purpose, and attached to the terminal on the pickup. Screw in a bulb, replace the roof and put the car back in service. Now the passengers can see again!

Most passenger cars came from the factory with one socket centrally located to light the interior. While single bulbs are adequate for most of them, large coaches like the 710 and 712 heavyweights need extra illumination. Special sockets are not necessary; an electronics supply company can provide economical bayonet-based ones and bulbs of the correct voltage rating to fit. Three bulbs inside one of these giants are just about right.

While American Flyer provided bulbs in many of its Prewar cabooses, Lionel's are uniformly dark and drear, but the same pickup rollers can be placed on 807, 657, 1722 and 817 models with ease. Window glazing heightens the effect, and can be installed as outlined near the end of Chapter Seven. Best of all, the addition of lights makes no permanent modification to a car. The socket and pickup can be removed at any time and the cross brace replaced in the truck to put the unit back in original condition.

Another nice touch is a pair of miniature bulbs behind the red marker light lenses on the observation platform of a 614 or 601. The photograph shows them in place on my restored Blue Comet. Why didn't Lionel do this?

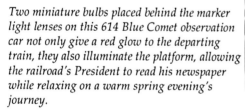

Two miniature bulbs placed behind the marker light lenses on this 614 Blue Comet observation car not only give a red glow to the departing train, they also illuminate the platform, allowing the railroad's President to read his newspaper while relaxing on a warm spring evening's journey.

Buildings should be lighted inside as well, and toggle switches can be wired into their circuits so that the bulbs can be turned on and off selectively. Chapter Twelve has further details. With the regular lights in the train room turned off, a layout should pulse and glow with lights and life of its own. The effect is magic!

We're making progress! The track is down and powered, the locomotives are hitched to their trains, and the cars are lighted to perfection. It's time to add more lights and action!

NINE

Trackside Accessories

Much of the charm of a toy train layout comes from little points of action triggered by the passage of the trains. Lights change from green to red and back again, gates descend, bells ring and the wonderful little gateman dashes from his shed to warn cars and pedestrians to keep clear of the tracks.

All of these devices are easy to add anywhere and at any time, provided the system has been wired with control rails as described in Chapter Six. Protruding beneath the layout are many green wires connected to the insulated control rails of the track. Any car or locomotive touching such a rail completes the ground and activates any trackside accessory wired to it.

Solenoid-operated crossing gates were a popular accessory with all manufacturers, and are readily available today. The 077 model in the photograph was produced by Lionel in various plain and lighted versions from 1923 through 1939. It operates reliably on 12 to 14 volts.

Built for use with both O and Standard Gauge trains, Lionel's 077 crossing gate operates by an efficient solenoid coil that pulls the arm down to a horizontal position as the train approaches, then allows it to rise again when the caboose or observation car has passed.

The prefix "0" in the catalog number of this and other early accessories indicated that it came with a section of O Gauge track outfitted with an insulated control rail. Without the "0" (as in a "77" crossing gate), a Standard Gauge track section was provided.

Power is supplied to the gate by means of one wire from a fixed voltage terminal on the transformer providing at least 12 volts. This should pass through a toggle on the control panel to allow the gate to be switched off if desired.

For the most realistic operation, the gate should descend while the train is still some distance from the crossing, but should rise again as soon as the last car passes. This is easy to accomplish if the trains al-

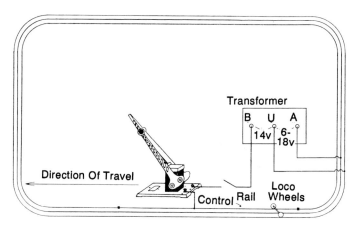

The crossing gate receives power through the 14-volt wire from the transformer when the toggle switch is closed, but will not operate until the circuit is grounded. This is accomplished when the wheels of any car or loco form a bridge between the ground rail and the control rail. As long as the toggle is on, any passing train will cause the gate to descend.

ways run in the same direction. One identifies the control rail three or more feet in advance of the crossing, and connects the ground wire from the gate to its green lead, as well as to the lead from the control rail in front of the gate. When the locomotive touches the first control rail, the ground is completed and the gate activated. It will stay down until the last car has moved from the end of the final control rail, as shown in the diagram.

If trains normally operate from either direction, control rails extending for a short distance on either side of the grade crossing should be selected. This will result in the gate staying down for a brief period after the last car passes. (Sophisticated detection devices now exist that can be wired to make the gate perform in prototypal fashion or from either direction, but these were not available prior to World War II, and therefore I choose not to use them. The insulated control rail method was developed by Lionel much earlier.)

Other accessories can be connected to the same type of circuit, such as the 45 gateman and Lionel's beautiful near-scale 46 single and 47 double crossing gates. To increase the illusion of distance that small accessories create, I use these near the back of the layout (regretfully, however, as their attractive appearance pleases me, and I'd like them to be easier to see.)

Earliest of all Lionel accessories with an animated figure (1935), the 45 gateman design is still available today, in plastic and under a new catalog number, from Lionel Trains, Inc. This Prewar version built of sheet metal operates by solenoid whenever the train approaches. A bulb in the base shines upward to make the plastic lantern in the figure's hand appear to glow.

A gate design more modern than the 077, lighted but still oversized, was introduced in 1940 and continued for several years after the war. This 152 model had a small pedestrian gate that worked by lever action from the main gate, and was painstaking to align; children (including myself in the '40s!) often removed it out of frustration. The appearance of the 152 gate is more realistic than the older type, and it operates well (if noisily) when properly adjusted.

The question of scale and size bears some examination. Most of the early trackside accessories were originally designed for use with Standard Gauge trains. For this reason, and because

This attractive accessory was built in much better proportion to the size of O Gauge trains than the 077 model, which was also used with Standard Gauge models. Even Lionel's Postwar gate designs were too large, but they operated reliably and were sturdy. These little versions are more delicate, and the fragile lantern baskets are often lost or broken. They may frequently require adjustment or repair, but are worth the effort.

large toys could be made to be sturdier, most are grossly out of proportion to O Gauge trains, as illustrated by the Lionel 080 semaphore in the photograph. I have used them on layouts in the past, but find them distracting; they detract from the overall impression of the display by commanding too much attention by virtue of their size alone.

The Standard Gauge accessories from the first third of the century were sold for use with O Gauge trains as well, but overpower them visually. If used at all, they should be placed near the front of the layout, as they destroy perspective when located at the back. This 080 semaphore could be wired into the track circuit to stop the train when the light was red, but had to be reset by hand. A similar model, the 082, contained an automatic device that would restart the locomotive after ten seconds or so. This device is explained in the discussion of the 078 train control signal on page 115, and in Chapter Eleven under stop stations.

The Ives 332 automatic bell signal shown later in this chapter is similarly out of scale, and I have not used it on the present layout, despite its pleasant antique appearance. It is a testament to the durability of these old toys, however, and will find a home on the small Standard Gauge layout I plan to build for my wife's burgeoning collection of these larger-sized toys.

Another outsized but appealing item is the 1045 watchman, which was first made in 1938. When wired to a very short control rail or a supplementary track contact as shown in the diagram, this giant figure waves his flag aggressively. I usually include him on my Christmas layout at the Acadia Band's holiday presentation, and he is so large that his frantic motion is visible to most of the audience from the stage.

This accessory cannot be wired to a regular control rail, as the flag will stay in a raised position throughout the passage of the train if subject to a continuous ground. Instead, it should be attached to a

The huge Lionel 1045 crossing watchman waves his flag to warn motorists and pedestrians alike when the train approaches.

A short control rail or a 1-inch contact plate provides an intermittent ground that waves the watchman's flag convincingly. An on-off switch should be provided in the circuit, and trains should not be left standing on the contact, as the wiring in this item is prone to overheating.

very short track section (approximately 1 inch) or to a metal plate lying on top of, but insulated from, the running rail. Each wheel that touches it triggers the waving action, but the flag drops when the wheel leaves the contact. Further details on this system appear in Chapter Six.

Lionel made alternately flashing highway warning signals as early as 1928. The model 79 was nearly a foot high and blinked by means of bimetallic strips (described in the discussion of train-stop stations in Chapter Eleven). It was replaced in 1940 by a crossbuck design numbered "154", two-thirds as high and much less bulky, with a more modern appearance. This signal depended upon the train wheels to complete the circuits for its flashing lights.

A special snap-on track contact was made to cause these crossbucks to flash, but the short ground rails on that device are too close together, making the blinking pattern highly uneven. An alternate method produced a still imperfect but somewhat more realistic rate of alternation. This system and an easy way of duplicating it are explained in Chapter Six.

High on my list of maddening devices are the warning bell signals that were made by all three companies under scrutiny here. Placed beside a grade crossing and wired to a control rail in the same manner as a crossing gate, they blast out a shrill ring that is as much buzz as bell.

Automobiles at grade crossings were protected from Lionel trains by this 154 flashing highway signal, beginning in 1940. The design was continued after the war. The authentic Prewar method of lighting the bulbs alternately involved insulated contacts placed on the rails where they completed the circuit when a train's wheels touched them.

The mechanism is much like an old-fashioned doorbell, with a make-and-break set of contacts powering a magnet that slams the clapper against the bell (or bells, in the case of Lionel's 069; talk about overkill!). Broken ones are very easy to repair, but I refuse to tell you how; consult an electrician if you must. Three revolutions of the track by a long streamliner, and I'm ready to chop them off at the base. Put an on-off switch into the circuit! Please!

Manufacturers often bought accessories from rival companies in the early years and sold them under their own trade names and catalog numbers. Lionel first sold stations of German manufacture, and later distributed those made by Ives before adding originals of their own. Both cars and accessories from Lionel were sold by American Flyer until a complete line was established by the Chicago company.

This was not surprising; much of Lionel's reputation from the early years through the 1960s was based upon the fun inherent in clever action accessories. This New Jersey firm led the way consistently with ingenious devices to

Judging by the number of these warning bell signals that were sold, children of Prewar days must have loved them. They are usually found in non-operating condition (made that way by deafened parents, no doubt!), but are extremely simple and easily repaired.

delight youngsters, and all can be examined in the early catalogs (reprinted by Greenberg's) and in the Train Collectors Association book entitled *Lionel Trains, Standard of the World, 1900-1943.*

The company offered tunnels, bridges, signals, buildings, lighted towers and telegraph poles, traffic signals and signal towers, stations and lamp posts and trackside items of all kinds, many of which had lights or action devices included. Some even moved the freight, as explained in Chapter Ten.

Usually the first to create action accessories for toy railroads, Lionel invented this block signal which stopped a train, then allowed it to continue after a brief interval, all automatically. It was marketed from 1924 through 1932, when a new version with a yellow caution light (099) replaced it.

One such item was the 078 train control, an oversized block signal that looked more like an old-fashioned traffic light and which contained bulbs that shone through red and green lenses. When wired into the power circuit to the track, this signal stopped the train when it entered an insulated block, and the light turned red. Inside, a bimetallic strip began heating, finally closing a contact that re-energized the track and allowed the locomotive to proceed, while simultaneously turning the light green. This circuit is shown in the diagram, and the concept of the bimetallic strip is further explored in Chapter Eleven.

Transformer

U 6- A
-18v-

Bimetallic Strip

Resistance Wire

Red

Green

Track

Loco Motor

Insulated Block

When no train occupied the insulated block, power was cut off from the resistance wire wrapping of the bimetallic strip, so that current did not reach the third rail. A train entering the block therefore stopped, but closed the circuit by means of a trickle of current through the locomotive motor and the resistance wire. This heated the strip, which then bent until the contacts closed to restart the locomotive. The whole process took about ten seconds (longer on the first try when cold), a realistic time for a train to pause in the area of a station. This device was later incorporated in several different stations, beginning in 1935.

One of the most durable types of trackside accessory was the lighted block signal without train control, made in two Prewar and several Postwar designs by Lionel from 1923 through 1969, and also by American Flyer and Ives. They contained two lights (red and green) which could be lighted alternately to indicate the presence of a train in a specific stretch (*block*) of track.

On a prototype road these signals were not lighted at all times, but only when triggered by trains in the appropriate areas. A green signal indicated clear track ahead, while red warned of an occupied block and signaled the engineer to slow or stop. American Flyer's 2218 model functioned in this way. Each of two special track sections with removable depressed fourth rails was wired to one of the bulbs, which lit when the train's wheel flanges touched them. Proper placement of these sections could duplicate the signaling pattern of a real railroad.

Any two-light block signal can be wired in this way, by means of our versatile control rails. The diagram shows a typical plan, wherein the signal shows green as the train approaches and turns to red after it passes.

These block signals contained one red and green bulb each, which lighted to show the presence or absence of a train in a designated section of main line. The Lionel models were numbered "069" (early) and "153" (late), while American Flyer's was 2218. The smaller 153 was continued after the war, then replaced by a highly realistic plastic design in the mid-1950s.

Lionel's 069 block signal worked from insulated control rails, as did gates and warning bells, but the later and more modern 153 design, introduced in 1940, was powered by a pressure-activated device that was placed under the ties. A spring on this device kept it elevated when no train was present, and the upper contacts lighted the green light. The weight of a passing train closed the lower contacts instead, and lit the red light. Contrary to prototype, one light or the other was always lighted.

I now admit to another digression from prototype practice: my block signals are lighted all the time. I like them that way! They also provide information for me, showing when my protected main line blocks are occupied, and in this way fulfill the same function as on the Santa Fe or New York Central. This is accomplished by connecting them to the train-control relays, as explained in Chapter Six.

Lionel built one item that served a valuable purpose besides decoration, although it provided no action and the lighting of its red bulb usually signified trouble. Early transformers contained

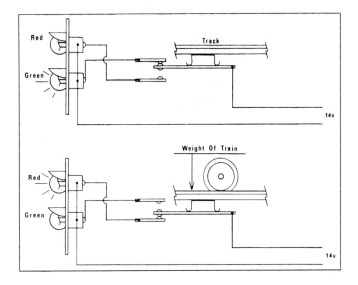

When connected in the manner shown, a block signal will turn from green to red as the train passes. A neutral section of track must be provided between the two control rails, equivalent to the normal length of trains in use on the line. If the two connected control rails are instead adjacent to each other, the green bulb will remain on for a while after the red one lights.

Unweighted track allows the upper contacts on the 153-C contactor to remain closed, leaving the green light of the block signal lighted. A passing train presses this device down, touching the bottom contacts together and lighting the red bulb instead. A spring adjusts the sensitivity of this device to accommodate differently weighted trains.

no safeguard against short circuits, and would burn out if left plugged in with their terminals shorted. This could happen easily if a train derailed while its young operator was out of the room.

When wired between the transformer and the track, Lionel's 91 circuit breaker reacted to an overload by opening the circuit, and also lighted the warning signal on top. It could be reset by hand once the problem with the train or wiring was resolved. Since modern transformers such as the Trainmasters have this protection built in, it is no longer necessary to use these separate items for their intended purpose, so I wire mine to remain lighted all the time. Placement outside my 436 power station contributes to a satisfying industrial appearance.

Another prosaic but useful item proves its worth on any layout with dead-end sidings. The 025 Lionel bumper fastens to the rails and lights up when power is present, letting the operator know if a siding is energized. Although its unyielding surface can put dents in fast-moving cars that strike it (it lacks the spring-loaded plunger of its Postwar successor), this handy device has more than once kept my equipment from hitting the scenery or floor.

One trackside accessory was engineer-operated rather than automatic, and was first introduced by American Flyer, one of the few accessories that Lionel did not come out with first. Prior to 1940, water towers were static devices used for decoration only, but with the advent of Flyer's 596 model in that year, young operators could lower the spout over a tender at the touch of a button. This accessory was continued after the war, when it was joined by Lionel's larger and more impressive models (one of which actually pumped water inside a transparent tank), but the 596 is the only operating water tower I know of with true Prewar credentials. The spout was powered by a solenoid, and the roof had a beacon light and a directional arrow to indicate "North" to passing aircraft.

Another item was developed by necessity. With its larger rival holding the patents on relay-activated whistles mounted in locomotive tenders, Flyer tried a four-rail whistle-blowing system for one year, then abandoned it and moved the whistle into a trackside billboard. These were decorated with advertising signs, including Royal Typewriters and the Ringling Brothers and Barnum and Bailey Circus, and were used after the war to promote the trains themselves. That version is shown here, although it is constructed in the same manner as the Prewar model, and I usually cover the picture of the diesel with an ad more appropriate to my railroad's era.

Used in conjunction with a 436 power station, the Lionel 91 circuit breaker resembles a typical piece of electrical generation equipment. It can still be used to provide protection for older transformers.

Lionel and Flyer whistles were similar, consisting of an air-tight sound chamber, a small electric motor and a fan-like impeller that forced air past a metal reed or lip at the external port. Two and even three different tones were produced at one time, and Flyer had one model with a solenoid-operated sliding panel that changed the tone of the whistle as it was sounding.

The motors of these whistles are serviced and repaired like those in locomotives. The sound chamber assembly usually needs little attention other than lubrication of the impeller shaft. However, the white metal castings sometime deteriorate or warp. Often a seemingly straight whistle box will change shape if the steel cover plate is removed. When this happens, the unit can not be reassembled in airtight condition. Even the slightest leak will keep the whistle from sounding. Nor can such distorted sound chambers be straightened again without fear of cracking.

These units can often be salvaged, however. The gasket that seals the cover plate is too thin to do the job if the casting is warped, but thicker and softer replacement gasket material can be obtained from any auto supply house, and will conform to the uneven contours of a malformed whistle well enough to seal in the air. A really thick layer may be needed, in which case longer screws must be used to replace the cover plate. Usually the impeller shaft rides in a bearing in the cover plate, but is long enough to fit even with a thicker gasket installed.

Lionel provided its customers with a variety of railroad and residential buildings to enhance a layout. One of my favorites is the little 092 signal "tower" (a misnomer, as the structure rests at ground level) with its many lighted windows. The body was borrowed from the elevated 438 version, but mounted on a low platform and sold for a lower price. Its small size makes it ideal for a distant location on the pike.

One of the few cases in which American Flyer scooped Lionel was the 1940 introduction of an operating water tower.

Although tender-mounted whistles are more realistic, clever young engineers can compensate by blowing the one in this billboard just as the locomotive passes by. Some of these Flyer accessories had base-mounted lights to illuminate the advertising signs. Automatic operation is also possible, by attaching the ground wire to a control rail located next to the billboard.

Small-scale items such as this 092 signal tower and 184 bungalow add interest to a layout, but must be carefully placed so that their undersized proportions contribute to, rather than detract from, the illusion of distance and perspective. They belong far away, which is unfortunate since they are very attractive.

Also small, in fact closer to HO size than O, were the various bungalows and manor houses provided for Lioneltown inhabitants. They were available separately or as part of elaborate scenic plots with trees, hedges and terraces. They work best at the back of a layout as contributors to a feeling of perspective. Placing them next to a 126 or 115 station is ludicrous.

Other examples of toy train accessories are visible in the various photos in this book: small Lionel and Flyer water towers, several kinds of bridges, static warning signs and lamp posts, and my favorite "cheaters" from the Postwar years, the 450 signal bridge, 394 rotating beacon, 395 floodlight tower and Lionel's handsome 138 water tower. Two specific categories deserve special attention, however, as they are fundamental to the spirit of railroads, both real and toy.

Trains were intended to be a means of transportation; they carry freight and passengers, and to do so they must be equipped to load and unload both. No railroad could therefore be complete without both kinds of stations, and the addition of Lionel's four most impressive accessories of the immediate Prewar period (three of which were freight-handlers) is an asset to capturing the flavor of the entire era. The next two chapters examine these gems.

TEN

Centerpiece ~ Lionel's Magnificent Four

T he Depression notwithstanding, Lionel must have been making money in the latter 1930s. Each new catalog featured a host of innovative models and features that moved the company steadily away from toy caricatures toward realistic representations of actual railroads. Tooling costs were high; preparations for the 700E Hudson consumed $75,000 before the first example could be sold, a huge investment in the as-yet untested market for mass-produced scale models in O Gauge.

Locomotive varieties proliferated. Streamlined Torpedos and Commodore Vanderbilts were joined by the Hiawatha and diesel passenger sets in every price range. Trains whistled and uncoupled by remote control, even in lower-priced sets with realistic die-cast locos that were much more thoroughly detailed than their sheet metal predecessors. From the bottom-line 1664 2-4-2 to the long and beautiful 2-6-4 226E with its twelve-wheeled tender, Lionel trains were becoming more and more like the real thing.

As observed earlier, my layouts rarely see anything more modern than a City of Denver or a Red Comet, although my childhood 229 gets an occasional outing for nostalgic reasons. The die-cast steamers so closely resemble Postwar production that I feel they compromise the Prewar atmosphere. By contrast however, four items from those turn-of-the-decade catalogs represent such a fundamental change of direction that they deserve inclusion. Even more important, they are great fun and make the best use of those fascinating new dumping freight cars.

1938 must have been a year of great uncertainty and concern. Europe was only a year away from war, and although the United States would not join the conflict until after the bombing of Pearl Harbor late in 1941, part of the North American continent was involved almost from the beginning; Canada entered in defense of Great Britain in 1939!

There was also considerable optimism. Plans for the 1939 World's Fair promised inconceivable advances in technology and living standards. Travel by air was becoming almost commonplace, and the automobile was considered a fairly dependable mode of personal transportation. The economic morass of the previous decade showed signs of fading, and because of the isolationist atmosphere that prevailed in the United States, many remained convinced that Nazi Fascism would remain primarily a European problem.

Concurrent developments in toy trains signaled the beginning of a fundamental change in the relationship between children and their playthings. Hands-on involvement had been the rule for years; imagination played a tremendous role, as young railroaders loaded their own barrels into gondolas, handled their own lumber, and generally provided their own mental images of the activities of their trains' supposed crew members and passengers.

Little more than a decade later, toy railroads would be peopled instead by animated, versatile figures and animals that brought to life the imagination of the '30s child. Cattle and horses moved in and out of stock cars, propelled not by little hands but by mechanical vibrations which were instigated by remote-control buttons. Milkmen actually delivered cans; freight handlers opened boxcar doors; cops pursued hoboes who dared steal a ride; and the proprietor of the poultry car actually swept his own floor!

Miniature machinery handled freight of all sorts. Logs rode on conveyor belts and rolled onto waiting cars. Coal cascaded from hoppers on an elevated ramp, ice was loaded into reefers, barrels rolled with the apparent assistance of a scale-sized worker, and a sawmill seemed to turn trees into finished boards.

It was a revolution in toy-making philosophy, profoundly affecting the lives of children ever since. And it all began with a Lionel idea in 1938!

Pictured on a page all its own in the 1939 catalog, the coal loader was Lionel's first remote-control freight handler. It came in three versions. The deluxe 97 had an endless chain of buckets driven by an electric motor, on the opposite side from a solenoid-operated delivery chute. The less expensive 96 had a hand crank for the bucket chain, but still released its stored load from a distance by electricity. Lacking the buckets, number 98 was the cheapest and had to be loaded by hand, but could still deliver the coal by remote control. The all-electric version stayed in the catalogs for several years after the war.

Coal Loader

Page 44 is my favorite in the 1939 Lionel catalog. It proudly displays the first all-remote-control mechanical loader ever offered in the toy train field, and a sophisticated entry it was. A powerful but noisy electric motor turned a shaft geared to an endless chain of miniature coal buckets that scooped the artificial anthracite from a tilting bin and toted it up to be stored. There

For the first time, beginning in 1938, juvenile engineers could watch their freight cars being filled and emptied without touching them at all. A remote-control button could be used to dump coal from the red and black car into the tower's receiving bin. Another control started the endless chain of buckets that hauled the coal to the storage area at the top of the unit, where it awaited a signal to open the chute on the opposite side to fill another car. When compared with today's electronic wizardry it seems tame and simple, but in 1938 it was magic!

it awaited delivery through the chute on the opposite side, held back by a hatch that opened by means of a solenoid.

This marvelous toy must have been a windfall for the company, for it required the purchase of extra equipment in order to function at its best. Since it loaded on one side and emptied on the other, it had to be placed between two tracks. For most buyers this necessitated the purchase of extra track and probably at least one switch to make a siding. Of course, a dump car was needed to get the coal into the receiving bin, and an uncoupling ramp was required to make it work. Lionel thoughtfully packaged these last two items together with the deluxe loader and a full pound of coal, in a special and relatively high priced set ($12.75 in 1939).

Lionel's drawing boards must have been busy. In addition to the scale and semi-scale switchers and freight cars, and the broad range of scale-detailed steamers and rolling stock that appeared in the last few years before the war, three big accessories debuted in 1940.

Log Loader

One worked on the same basic principle as the coal loader. The 164 log loader was positioned between two tracks placed about 15 inches apart, as measured between the center rails. Its slanted receiving bin guided logs to a pair of endless chains equipped with rounded log-catchers that carried the cargo up and over the top into a storage area. It was great fun to watch! The logs dropped over the top with a satisfying crash, rolled first one way and then the other down a pair of switch-back inclines, and finally came to rest against two stakes. A solenoid dropped the stakes on command, so that the logs could roll off into any waiting lumber car or gondola.

The mechanisms of both the coal and log loaders are not too complex and are easy to service. If kept properly lubricated, the gears are extremely durable and last a long time. While permanent layout installation tends to discourage this routine maintenance, since the units must be turned over for access to the machinery, any sounds of protest from dry shafts or gears should not be ignored. Mishandling sometimes results in broken coal buckets, lost lumber stakes or broken chains, but all are available as reproductions. Even replacement control boxes are

Logs from the automatic lumber car are carried up under the roof and dumped on the other side, where they rest against stakes until the operator drops them into another waiting car.

presently being manufactured, although they take up a lot of room on the control panel, and I have devised a substitute.

A simple toggle switch can be used to activate the motors that drive the chains in either accessory. A normally "open" push button is used to dump the cargo from the storage areas, and a second toggle can be wired to light the two bulbs beneath the log loader's red Bakelite roof.

It is easy to identify the wires leading to each of these controls by tracing them to where they are attached to the motor, bulb or solenoid terminals.

Magnetic Crane

One toy for which I have retained the original controller is the 165 magnetic crane, also placed on the market for the 1940 season. While its ingenious mechanism can be operated by an assortment of toggles or push buttons, Lionel's controller manages to do it all compactly and well.

The operating mechanism is far more complex than in the previously described toys. The cab is mounted on an axle which allows it to rotate in either direction, and the hook is attached to a cord wound around a drum. One motor powers all operations. Pushing any of the control buttons starts the motor, but depending upon which one is touched, a solenoid shifts a complex gear cluster to turn the cab right or left, or send the hook up or down.

A simple rotary switch in the center is turned to activate the magnet, also lighting a red bulb in the cab. In practice, the magnet is lowered over a pile of scrap metal and turned on. Pieces adhering to the magnet can be hoisted and swung in any direction, then

Four buttons on a compact control box govern the motion of both cab and hook on Lionel's 165 magnetic crane, and a knob in the middle turns the magnet on and off. A single non-reversing motor turns the cab left or right and raises or lowers the hook through a system of gears, engaged by a solenoid-operated transmission. When the magnet is energized, a red light glows in the cab.

released by turning the magnet off. In this manner, gondola cars may be loaded from a trackside pile or unloaded the same way, or cargo may be shifted from one car to another.

This accessory needs frequent lubrication, a difficult task if it is fastened permanently to a layout, as the top plate must be unscrewed to provide access to the motor. Fortunately it is a tough toy, and can withstand a lot of abuse and neglect. The example shown here was found in badly damaged condition, and the gears appeared to have been run dry, but it was restored using all original parts, and still functions beautifully.

Any grinding noise from the gearbox indicates the need for some grease. The motor is noisy, but the sound of dry gears is higher in pitch and very distinctive; it should not be ignored. Another minor problem can occur with the wiring. If a spark occurs when the magnet touches a metal car on the tracks, reverse the ground and power leads to the crane. This situation is caused by current in the casing of the magnet flowing directly to the grounded body of the car.

These beautiful toys delight visitors as much as they do their owner, and should be located close to the viewing area of a layout, and not too far from the operator. Their action is most effective when seen from close up, and they exert endless fascination for youngsters especially. Earlier I mentioned my little friend Heather, and her tendency to dump the coal before a car could be spotted beneath the chute. She isn't the only such offender! More than once I have been known to hit the wrong button, sending an avalanche of logs rolling across the countryside. (The logs are easier to clean up than the coal, of course.)

Bascule Bridge

The fourth item in this category seems to be everyone's favorite, the immense 313 bascule bridge. It moves no freight, and it only goes up and down, but its beauty, sheer size and realistic appearance guarantee enduring popularity.

The bridge was made both before and after the war, and the mechanism was redesigned in 1945. The lifting section is very heavy, and is operated by a small motor and gearbox. The Prewar version relied heavily upon the gears, with the help of a powerful spring located in one of the towers which was designed to lessen the strain on the motor. Because the tension of the spring tended to distort the framework, many of these toys are found today in warped or broken condition. After the war the spring-assist system was reworked to ease the strain.

Although a prototypical counterweight box was located on the back of the bridge, it was empty. In restoring the mechanism, I placed a quantity of lead in this box to help balance the bridge and prevent further pressure on the frame. Consequently the spring must no longer be tightened excessively to raise the span, and it operates more quietly.

The example shown in the photograph was rusted and bent, with a broken frame and a frozen gearbox, but it responded to

The 313 bascule bridge introduced by Lionel in 1940 is, in the author's opinion, the most impressive operating accessory ever produced. While well-preserved examples are very expensive today, restoring a damaged one for layout use is a rewarding project for the economy-minded engineer.

simple restoration techniques and functions well today. There is no substitute for the quality materials and good basic design that such firms as Prewar Lionel displayed in abundance.

The bridge was sold with a special frame to align it with the approach track at the end of the span that raises and lowers; this frame often became separated from the bridge, and is frequently missing today. The rails on the end of the bridge are open at the bottom, and fit closely over the approach track when the lift span descends. When installed permanently on a layout, the alignment frame is not required; accurate placement of the receiving track will ensure smooth operation. The structure should be fastened securely to the table to eliminate excess vibration and prevent warping of the frame.

Mechanically, the drive system is simple. A non-reversing motor turns a series of gears to raise and lower the bridge in a continuous cycle, although an on-off switch added to the circuit will allow the operator to stop it at the top. Electrically it is more complex. Cam-driven sets of contacts (leaf switches) open and close at various points in the operation. A touch of the control button starts the sequence, closing one leaf switch that maintains power to the motor even if the button is released. Another switch opens as the bridge begins to rise, cutting off the current feed to the track on either side of the bridge to stop the train. As the bridge descends again, these switches reverse themselves, shutting the motor off automatically and restoring power to the track.

Since the bridge must be wired to the track to stop the trains and prevent possible accidents, reverse units must be deactivated, or the locomotives will be left standing in neutral when current is restored. Adding three ohms of resistance into the circuit will preserve the automatic reversing feature. This circuit is included in the accompanying diagram, and is further explained in Chapter Six.

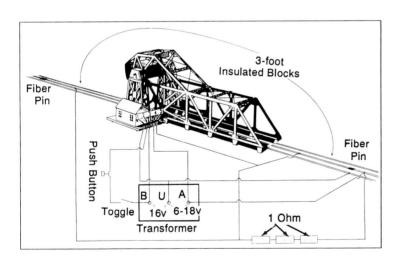

When wired as shown, Lionel's 313 bascule bridge will complete its cycle automatically at the touch of a single button. The on-off toggle switch is provided to allow the bridge to be stopped at the top of its rise, as the internal leaf-spring contacts keep the motor operating all the way to the end of the sequence, even after the starter button is released. Similar contacts shut off power to the approach tracks on either side of the bridge, but automatic reversing can be maintained by wiring three 10-watt, 1-ohm resistors into the circuit as shown.

Two versions of the Prewar bascule bridge can be found, one with gray-painted girders and the other painted silver. The revised model produced after the war has an aluminum bridge and some slight modifications in the structure to accommodate the improved spring mechanism.

Lionel's four magnificent operating accessories can be the main focal point for a display-oriented toy train layout. Their functional appearance and operational potential capture the technological atmosphere that was only just beginning to be represented in toys around 1940, a trend that would come to symbolize the entire second half of the twentieth century. As a collective centerpiece for a Prewar toy train empire, they are unsurpassed. See color photo 29.

Now that we've moved the freight, it's time to provide for our passenger traffic.

ELEVEN

Stations ~ Active and Passive

N o other toy train accessory has been produced in such a variety of sizes, shapes and colors as the passenger station. Logically placed stations are fundamental to a convincing layout, giving the trains a starting point and a destination, and serving as a focal point for miniature towns, just as the prototypes did for many American communities from the mid-1850s onward.

In addition to their decorative purpose, functional stations have provided young engineers with hidden transformers, auxiliary whistles and train-stop devices to enhance overall realism. With wide-ranging price tags reflective either of their simplicity, their technical components or an almost baroque ornamentation, stations of some sort were within almost everyone's grasp, and many have survived the ravages of time and children alike.

Ives pioneered the building of these miniature depots in the United States, offering lithographed beauties at least as early as 1903. Most spectacular were the glass-canopied platforms that covered one or more tracks and were used in conjunction with both freight and passenger buildings. While most were sold to accompany Ives trains, the firm also distributed these products through other manufacturers, most notably Lionel from 1906 until about 1916. Lionel stations were made by Schoenhut from 1917 to 1920.

Both American Flyer and Lionel purchased their earliest stations from German toymakers in the first decade of the century, and continued to offer them until World War I interfered with their production and distribution. All sizes were marketed, but since Lionel was most heavily oriented toward large-sized models, most of their stations look best with Standard Gauge trains. The average Flyer design more closely matched their O Gauge line, the only size trains they produced prior to 1925.

In choosing stations for a layout, an operator faces the same problems as with rolling stock: lithographed examples are nearly impossible to restore, and undamaged ones bring high prices at train meets. By contrast, the enameled versions can be made to look like new much more easily.

This "Flyertown Depot" of 1924 was typical of thousands of small lithographed designs sold with American Flyer clockwork train sets from 1909 through 1933. The earliest were imported from Germany, and the same catalog number (in this case 90) was applied to a wide variety of styles.

Unless one specializes in stations, the accumulation of a large number is not likely to be a high priority. They take up a lot of room on a layout or on display shelves, and having too many on a layout is illogical from an operational point of view.

I have eight passenger and two freight stations on my present layout, reflecting my preference for passenger trains. This is probably too many, but they are scattered about and perform a variety of duties: two of them whistle, three stop the trains, and one even talks! With so many to choose from, I elected to maintain some unity of style by using Lionel designs primarily. My layout seems to have developed an overall '30s flavor, and to my eye they fit in the best.

Passenger Stations

After abandoning both Ives and German-made products, Lionel produced six definitive sizes of passenger stations. The two smallest types were intended only for O Gauge layouts, but the four largest were promoted for use with either O or Standard Gauge trains. In the case of the 112 and 126 types, the size discrepancy is not too noticeable, but the huge windows and doors on the 124 and the immense dimensions of the 114 make them seem appropriate for the larger scale only.

Except for the smallest, each size had a label indicative of the type of community it was intended to serve: "Lionel City" for the three big models; "Lionelville" for the mid-sized variety; and "Lioneltown" for the next-to-smallest type. While they bore a variety of catalog numbers, one number has been chosen here to represent each type, for purposes of convenience. See color photo 30.

First to appear after discontinuance of the German and Ives models was the 124-type Lionel City station (1920), measuring 13½ inches long by 9 inches wide and standing a full 13 inches tall. Other catalog numbers used for this size were 121, 122 and 123, indicating variously the presence or absence of interior and exterior lights. The company also produced an oval terrace 31½ inches long, complete with flower beds, lamps posts and a flag. It made a magnificent centerpiece for a Standard Gauge layout.

The Train Collectors Association lists nine different color and trim combinations for the 124 type. All but one had a green roof, and the walls ranged from brown and tan shades to orange. It was made through 1936, after which the catalog number changed to 134 to signify the addition of the train-stop mechanism. These large stations were available until the war.

Next came the first No. 126 Lionelville model in 1923. In this 10¼" x 7¼" x 7" model, the compromise between gauges worked. Although the windows and doors seem slightly oversized for O Gauge, the building's proportions blend well with the trains, and for this reason I chose the red and green 126 for my layout, but it also looks good with Standard Gauge trains.

Eleven different color combinations are known, some of them with sidewalls lithographed to represent brick, and others with a crackle enamel finish somewhat resembling painted stucco. A single bulb illuminated the interior; the otherwise identical 125 was unlighted, and was offered only through 1925.

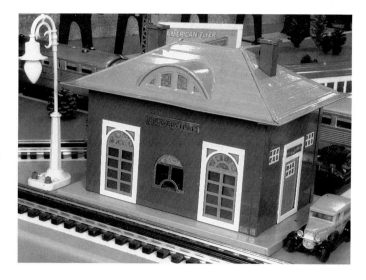

Arched window frames, rounded dormers and a ticket window identify the 126-type Lionel station, built from 1923 to 1936. This station was continued until the war as number 136 with automatic train control.

Third and smallest of the 1920s models, the 127 Lioneltown was intended only for O Gauge use. Thirteen variations are known, according to the Train Collectors Association. Walls ranged from white to mustard, and roofs were always some shade of red, but the windows and bases differed widely. The chimney can be found in lithographed brick or enameled yellow or white, and the nameplates are either brass or nickel.

I like to use this size in the middle to far distance for purposes of perspective. It looks best when serving small locos and cars. Like its larger cousins, the 127 received a new number (137) when the train-stopper was added in 1936, and a few were even sold after World War II, although they were probably leftovers and not newly manufactured. An interesting comparison of the size differences between these three types appeared in some of Lionel's catalogs. See color photo 31.

In 1931 the "Lionel City" name was applied to another style, the 112 type. This modern urban design had steel walls embossed to look like limestone, featured details such as a clock face and removable skylight, and was lighted. An otherwise identical 113 had two exterior light fixtures flanking the entrance.

Although its doors easily accommodated Standard Gauge-sized people, the proportions of this building are satisfactory when used in conjunction with O Gauge trains. Under catalog number 115, it was offered through 1949, long after Standard Gauge had been discontinued. The dimensions of its base were almost the same as the 124 type, allowing it to be used with the 129 terrace. It stood 8½ inches tall.

An immense station of the same basic design, but with an added wing on each side, appeared the same year, numbered 114. The base was 19¾ inches long, and it contained two interior and two exterior lights. Both of these large city stations were ivory colored with green trim and maroon doors, and were revised with new catalog numbers, colors, and the train-stop device in 1935. The 114 was no longer offered after the war. See color photo 32.

Lionel produced an eminently sensible group of accessories in 1935: stations that caused trains to stop in front of them, wait a short interval, and then resume their journeys. These train-stop devices were added to all four types of stations, which were thereafter offered in new and fewer colors.

The mechanism depended upon a bimetallic strip, the simple device that is at the heart of a thermostat. Two bands of metal with differing rates of thermal expansion are fused at the ends, and wrapped with a coil of resistance wire. When the wire is heated by a current passing through it, one side of the band expands faster than the other, causing it to bend. An electrical contact is located such that the strip bends to touch it when heated, thus completing a circuit.

In Lionel's mechanism, power to an insulated section of track in front of the station was routed through the bimetallic strip. Since the strip was usually straight, and not touching its contact, the circuit remained open and the track section was electrically dead. When a locomotive entered this section, it stopped.

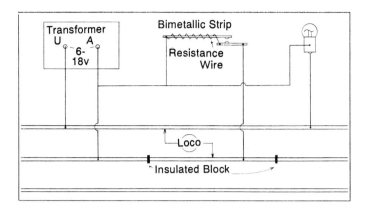

An insulated track section in front of the train-stop station is wired through the mechanism and does not receive power, as shown. This stops a loco's motor when it enters this section, but the resistance wire is then energized by a trickle of current through the motor, and begins to heat. When the temperature rises enough to bend the bimetallic strip over to close the circuit, the train restarts. According to John G. Hubbard in his book on repairing Prewar Lionel trains, an earlier alternate method heated the resistance wire through an insulated control rail when the loco entered the isolated block.

The presence of a locomotive on this track, however, sent a small amount of power through its motor to the coil of resistance wire, as shown in the diagram. The coil heated, the bimetallic strip bent, the circuit closed and the train restarted, as if by magic. A lever on the train control was accessible either on top of the urban station's flat roof, or beneath a removable roof on the other sizes. This lever adjusted the distance between the bimetallic strip and its contact, thus varying the length of time the circuit would stay open. Trains could be set to stop for long or short periods, or not at all. The E-unit had to be turned off in those locomotives with automatic reversing, or they would be left standing in neutral when the power was restored.

Placement of the insulated track section is critical for a realistic sequence of operation, and is dependent upon the direction of travel. Ideally, it should be arranged so that the locomotive enters the dead spot when the cars are in front of the station.

All three sizes of stop stations work busily on my layout. A big 117 Lionel City is located near the front, commanding my most heavily settled area. Resplendent in beige and light red, it was actually the economy model of the period, but is less commonly found today than its sister 115, which had lights on either side of the entrance doors. Trains on loop two are controlled by the 117, with the block-protecting relays turned off when it is in operation. One train per loop is the norm when the stop stations are functioning, to avoid rear-end collisions.

Mid-sized number 136, with its creamy yellow walls and red trim, stops the trains near the river, just before they plunge into the tunnel beneath the mountain. The insulated section is placed so as to stop most average-sized locomotives with their tenders beneath the water tower spout and their cars at the station door. It's great fun to stand back and watch visitors' faces when they discover that I'm not running the trains, but that they are somehow stopping and starting themselves with great precision.

Lionel's 117 station of 1935 to 1942 caused trains to pause in their journeys, allowing passengers to alight and board in comfort.

Down by the riverside, Lionel station number 136 stops a train with the tender lined up for servicing beneath the water tower spout. These stations were less varied in color than their predecessor 126s, but still came in four different shades of yellow. All had green bases and red roofs.

The little 137 toward the rear of my layout contains the same mechanism as its larger counterparts, and regulates trains on the elevated loop. The operator has a visual check on the operation of these devices, since the light inside glows brighter when the locomotive enters the insulated block, and dims slightly when the heated strip closes the circuit.

This accessory was cataloged in 1946 and was apparently sold after the war. However, it is assumed that only Prewar leftovers were available, and it was deleted from the line when supplies were exhausted. Lionel was primarily occupied with building various navigational and technical devices for the government from 1942 to 1945, and while some design work on trains was pursued during those years (most notably the new knuckle coupler), there seems to have been some indecision over what Prewar items to retain for the new line when the war was over. The big 115 station, 97 coal loader, 164 log loader and 313 bascule bridge all survived through 1949 or '50, but other accessories were dropped as the company moved toward newer and more realistic attractions.

Smallest of the train-stoppers, the 137 is a good candidate for back-of-the-layout locations. Its small size increases the illusion of distance, especially if it serves small steamers, electrics and rolling stock.

The tiny lithographed model that completes Lionel's passenger station line-up did triple duty. Measuring only 5½" x 3¾" and less than 4 inches high, it came in few color combinations with no added trim, but bore several catalog numbers. In one incarnation it housed a low-powered transformer for Winner, Lionel-Ives and Lionel Junior sets, some containing built-in rheostats. Another version was empty, and came with various clockwork and electric sets. The third version, however, is the one that has found a home in two locations on my layout.

When listed as 48W, the little lithographed station contained a whistle. It was available from 1937 until the war. It can be operated by push button or attached to a control rail for automatic actuation by any passing train.

These thin-steel toys are rarely found in good shape. The red lithographed roofs with an imitation shingle pattern are frequently rusted, and both of mine have been repainted. Many thousands were sold, and often relieved of their whistle motors, but even without the works inside they serve as good wayside stations for distant locations.

Like most of its kind, this Lionel 48W whistling station was rusty and battered when found, but its durable whistle responded to simple cleaning and works just like new. Lionel made tough toys!

Mystic Talking Station

My final passenger station also has a freight bay, with loading ramp and cargo door. It is easily the most interesting and ingenious representative of the American Flyer company that I currently use on the layout. It talks!

A. C. Gilbert brought to American Flyer a fresh and creative approach that was both aesthetic and technological, and would eventually result in the slim and graceful S Gauge trains that competed with Lionel well into the 1960s. One of the first accessories introduced by the new management was the a-Koostikin talking passenger and freight station of 1939.

The strange name was dropped after the first year. Apparently meant to convey the concept of "acoustics," the title probably did little to help sell the product. It was introduced on pages 4 and 5 of the 1939 catalog, in a display that extolled its features and reported the receipt of an award for "outstanding achievement in toy construction for 1939" from a national toy buyer's association. The photo also showed the new 4-8-4 Union Pacific steamer.

In appearance, the station represented a major departure from previous Flyer and Lionel production. Its proportions were much more realistic, with a low profile and bi-level platform to accommodate both people and cargo. Colors were subdued: muted shades of cream and brown, with a light green roof and red chimney, all mounted on a gray base. The Postwar version appeared in bright red and white, but this early model seems much more convincing.

Nameplates on the roof ends read "Mystic", probably suggested by that Connecticut town near where the A. C. Gilbert firm was located in New Haven, but the title was also appropriate to the magical nature of the station's performance.

The mechanism was both simple and ingenious. A vertically mounted electric motor turned a 4⅝-inch phonograph record mounted beneath the floor and protected by a round metal plate. Only a small portion of the record was exposed through a rectangular hole in the station floor. Inside, a small round phonograph head was suspended by offset axle ends to swing between two metal supports. It looked much like the tone arm of any early Victor or Columbia acoustic

A simple, free-swinging acoustic sound reproducer played the record in American Flyer's a-Koostikin talking station. Thanks to a clever mechanism, the train stopped in front of the station to allow the recorded announcement to be heard: "The Continental Limited! All aboard! This train for New York, Philadelphia, Washington, Chicago, Denver, San Francisco and all points west! 'Board!" Sounds of a steam locomotive accompanied the voice.

phonograph, containing a vibrating diaphragm and a replaceable steel needle that rode in the record grooves.

A cam geared to the motor shaft controlled a series of leaf switches. When activated by an approaching train running over a track trip, the motor started its cycle and cut off power to the track, much the same as the arrangement in the Lionel bascule bridge described in the previous chapter. Another switch lighted the interior light, and the phonograph needle dropped onto the beginning of the record to begin its announcement.

At the end of the cycle, the needle was lifted out of the grooves. Because of the offset axles on the head, it swung back toward the beginning of the record, ready for the next performance, and the cam opened one contact to shut the station down and closed another to start the train. Kids must have loved it! According to visitors, it's the second most popular item on my layout today, surpassed only by the bascule bridge.

Because of the relatively delicate nature of the works, these stations are seldom found in good operating condition. The motor and gears were well made, however, and the phono head can usually be repaired. Replacement records are available that duplicate the original sounds. I use a replacement, in order to preserve the surface of my original copy.

Well proportioned and realistic in its Prewar colors, American Flyer's Mystic station looks as good as it sounds.

My a-Koostikin was found for me by a dealer friend, Tony Hay of Huntington, West Virginia, and was in near-perfect condition. I have never seen one so well preserved for sale at any train meet. (In my opinion, one of the best arguments for trading with dealers is their access to a greater number of obscure items than an average collector can ever hope to see, and the best ones keep track of their customers' wants and try to fulfill them.)

Because of its location on my mountain loop, which is wired in a complex fashion for automatic three-train operation, I do not employ the train-stop feature and have wired the station directly to a toggle switch on the control panel. It must be turned off by hand when the record reaches the end; the light goes out as a reminder. It is easy to install another bulb inside if constant illumination is desired, but I like the way the light commands attention when the sound begins. Visitors like to know where to look!

The best location for this station is the near mid-range of the layout. Its compromise dimensions (appropriate for either O or S Gauge trains) make it look undersized in the foreground, but it must be close enough to be heard distinctly. All of the trains can always be brought to a complete halt while its record plays, of course, but keeping it reasonably near the front allows it to be heard over the sounds of a train moving on another loop. It's more realistic that way.

Freight Stations

By now you will have seen that my passengers are guaranteed every possible comfort and convenience; the freight isn't so lucky!

One of only a few destinations for cargo on a passenger-oriented railroad is this metal platform of unknown heritage, constructed of sheet metal with cast roof supports. The Lionelville sign (added by the author) gives it a touch of class!

It must be the lights that attract me, for passenger cars are run much more frequently than cargo carriers on my railroad, and aside from the big accessories that service the dump cars, only two freight platforms and one kit-built industry give the freight trains somewhere to go. One of these platforms is a mystery to me; it came with the purchase of a Postwar set several years ago, its paint flaking and numerous dents pocking its surface. It carries no identification but is definitely elderly, and I've added a Lionelville sign to give it a little respectability.

The other freight platform is a Postwar plastic 157 whose days are numbered. It is located at the back, and will someday be replaced by its Prewar equivalent 156 with the older Bakelite base and roof, when I can find one. Lionel also made a big metal 155 for use with Standard Gauge trains, but it overwhelms O Gauge equipment.

Operators with a passion for freight are encouraged to investigate the stations made by American Flyer during the 1920s and '30s. Some were exclusively for cargo, while others were combination passenger and freight designs. Two types had hand-operated cranes, borrowed first from the 3025 wrecker car and later from the little ³⁄₁₆-inch version.

Ives made some attractive freight platforms as well, with elaborately lithographed roofs and as many as eight supporting columns. These date from the earliest years of the century to the mid-'20s, after which the new management sold Lionel stations under the Ives name. The firm also produced various stations with sliding baggage and cargo doors during the early years. This type of station creates an impression of antiquity quite unlike the 1930s style of the Lionel products.

This brief survey has barely scratched the surface. Many other companies produced every conceivable type of station during the Prewar period, and the variety that came from American Flyer alone (including especially the huge wooden Union Station with its clock tower and ornamental eagles) would fill a large layout with charm and appeal. There's something available for every taste and budget.

It appears that we have now accounted for all of the major components of our toy train empire: design, power, tables, track, engines, cars and accessories. It's time now to pull it all together.

TWELVE

Scenery ~
Realism vs. Impressionism

My previous modeling efforts in HO scale had as their primary goal the creation of an exact representation of the real world in miniature form. For hours I pored over the pages of *Railroad Model Craftsman* and *Model Railroader*, studying techniques of recognized masters and talented newcomers. More hours were consumed in hand-laying code 70 track, carefully weathered and with four spikes per tie. Turnouts had to be hand-built for realism; ballast had to match in color and consistency the gravel used on the nearby Dominion Atlantic branch of the Canadian Pacific.

Endlessly I searched for ways to reproduce grass and foliage, trying lichens, ground foam and even dried weeds. Patiently I mixed and blended dyes and paints to get just that slightly parched look of Nova Scotia lawns in August. Minuscule red apples were sprayed throughout simulated Cortland and MacIntosh orchards, and reminders of the recent passage of horses decorated the dirt streets of my towns.

One day I found myself contemplating the possibility of two HO scale lovers, plucking from a microscopic daisy its sub-atomic petals: "She loves me, she loves me not." Clearly I was drawing near to the boundaries of sanity! So much close focusing turned my eyes permanently inward, literally and figuratively. An agonizing crick in my neck made me resemble old Ebenezer Scrooge bent over his ledgers. And each new magazine issue sent me back to the train room, muttering about weathering and kitbashing and prototype accuracy.

There must be a touch of insanity in model railroaders, just as in artists of all types; why else would we expend so much time and energy in a Lilliputian world? But scale modeling is nothing if not an art form, the representation and preservation of human achievement in miniature. Perhaps we seek a form of permanence, of immortality, through the creation of an enduring masterpiece in tiny form.

Modelers the world over were saddened by the death of John Allen some years back; the subsequent destruction by fire of his amazing Gorre & Daphetid Railroad was equally tragic. The excellence of his life's work was worthy of preservation, and though the layout is gone, we are fortunate to have a permanent record, thanks to his skill as a commercial photographer. As yet, few scale layouts have been accorded the honor of becoming museum pieces, although the day may come.

Once I was nearly obsessed with this concept of permanence. Each street and lawn and coal pile and sand pit that I added to the layout would surely be there in fifty or a hundred years, examples of something concrete and unchanging in this world. But reality meant change, and each new job opportunity or study leave meant a change of address, a new home. Whenever I was sure that I had finally arrived at some permanent station in life, a new temptation peeked over the horizon. To change is to live; resisting change is to let life pass by.

And moving meant dismantling the railroad!

Destroying the results of painstaking hours, whether by choice or by necessity, was never easy. Yet I had finally arrived at the realization that my pleasure came not from the possession, but from the creation. Each completed layout was forgotten, lost in the planning of something new and stimulating to challenge my imagination. Into this stage of my life came the beautiful little Ives set from my father-in-law, and scale modeling was abandoned.

My respect and admiration for John Allen and his kind are boundless; they are true artists who inspire us all to greater accomplishments. But theirs is not the only approach. The preservation of our toy heritage is another worthwhile branch of this great hobby, and the creation of landscapes compatible with these toys is a fulfilling and laudable undertaking.

Toy trains vary from highly realistic to humorous caricatures, with most falling somewhere in between. They are generalized impressions of the real thing, serving to stimulate the minds and imaginations of children and adults alike. They belong in their own setting. To me, a Lionel 254 box cab electric is simply out of place among correct-to-the-inch buildings and scenery. The overall impression is wrong.

"Impression" is the key word! Most toys are interpretations of real objects, and in the case of trains, a setting to showcase them is an impression of the world they inhabit. The layout itself is not real; it is also a toy!

The original juvenile owners of most of our antique treasures did not build for the ages. They dismantled and rearranged their sectional track with great regularity, always seeking some new route for their metal monsters to follow, carrying with them their dreams. My toy layouts are prompted by the same motivation; they serve to expand my horizons, and are replaced as soon as they no longer fulfill this purpose.

Since they do not represent countless hours spent in carving ditches, molding tree trunks and tracing rust streaks below every nut and bolt, dismantling these layouts causes no soul-searching, and only a twinge of regret. They continue to exist in memory, and in photographs carefully stored away, but to build is the thing! To contemplate what one has built is fruitless vanity, unless it serves to guide one in future and better building!

A famous composer of music was once asked to name his favorite among his own works. His answer was, "The next one."

Creating the Impression

Now faced with self-imposed guidelines, I bravely present my approach to toy train scenery. The limitations are as follows: to create an impression of reality, rather than the reality itself; to create an appearance and atmosphere congruent with the nature of the toys; and to achieve the most appropriate ends with the greatest possible economy of time. Here is how I did it.

Before the track was laid, I painted the table with a base coat of tan semi-gloss latex. This now becomes the color of my roadbed, as well as dirt paths and river banks, and any other spot requiring an earth color. Overpainting provides other aspects of the scenery, most importantly an impression of grass. The trackage is first outlined and protected with masking tape, as shown in the accompanying sequence of photographs. It helps if you have already decided the location of major buildings, as paths to their doors can be masked at this time as well (a 1-inch strip is a perfect size for a footpath).

Why don't I ballast the track? There are three reasons — moisture, mess and maintenance. Gravel ballast must be glued in place, and while waterless contact cement can be used, the best

Masking tape used to outline the roadbed and to define any desired areas of dirt allows the modeler to paint grass quickly and easily, with a relatively large brush. When the tape is removed, neat edges set off the contrasting areas.

results are obtained with a mixture of white glue, water and a little detergent (see the various books on scenery techniques in any hobby store). Water is poison to toy trains; rust forms faster than a speeding bullet!

Equally important are the mess this procedure makes and the maintenance required to keep the ballast where it belongs. Even the most thorough gluing leaves some loose particles to foul the points of switches at a later date. And with an average life span of a year or so for each of my layouts, scraping off miles of solidified gravel each time I rebuild is a task I can do without!

Does painted roadbed look as realistic as ballast? Nope! But it does give the proper impression, and the tan color sets off the dark brown Gargraves ties nicely.

Once the tape has outlined the track and fields, green paint is applied. No artistry is required; the masking tape will protect the areas that are to remain tan. Two or three coats will cover nicely and protect the surface, and when the tape is removed the roadbeds and paths appear like magic.

If trackside signals are already installed, or if their intended locations are known, dirt areas can be provided around them before the grass is painted in. If not, it's easy to add them later. A little masking tape on the grass and two coats of tan paint will do the job.

Gray paint (not black) makes a convincing representation of asphalt streets. The white lines are strips of flexible artist's tape.

What color makes the best grass? I like a fairly bright green with more than a touch of yellow. It isn't realistic; most grass is variegated in shades of muted green and brown. But it gives the impression of grass, while at the same time providing a showcase for the brightly enameled trains and buildings. It looks right, if not real. It fits in well with the toys.

Providing for Traffic

Streets and sidewalks are created the same way, using gray paint to simulate asphalt. Letraline artist's tape ⅛-inch wide makes quick and easy curbs and traffic lines (white for a Prewar layout; yellow lines are a Postwar development!). A little planning in advance allows provision for trackside buildings, gates and other signals that also sit on pavement.

Elevated Scenery

While a railroad can be built entirely on a flat surface, the addition of mountains is a great asset, adding interest, depth and a relief from too many horizontal lines. Conventional methods of mountain-making produce excellent results, and range from the venerable chicken wire-and-plaster technique to hard-shell methods (in those hobby store books again) and commercial products. You shouldn't be surprised to discover I do it differently.

My mountains are almost weightless, easy to build in any shape and equally easy to change at any time. They adapt well to the needs of the track plan, fit in almost effortlessly around tunnel portals, and can even survive the attack of a tunnel-dwelling cat, as you will see. Their walls can be either thick or thin, and providing internal clearance for the trains is an easy part of the building process. The tops of my mountains are also quite thin, which proved to be fortunate on one notable occasion.

The Eruption of Mount Socrates

Pets and model railroads do not mix. Furry friends and iron horses should never occupy the same stable, as the results are likely to be disastrous. Fishing hamsters out of culverts or parakeets out of bridges can be annoying, but most catastrophic of all was the eruption of Mount Socrates.

Our household supports two or three assorted cats at any given time. The Chairman of the Board is Chessie, a beautiful gray and white female who looks like she stepped right out of the Chesapeake & Ohio Railroad logo. Her pursuits run more to rodents than railroads, but the same cannot be said for my wife's number one feline, Socrates.

Socs is a lovely long-haired black and white of assorted parentage, possibly the most affectionate cat ever born. No lap is foreign territory to her, and she makes you feel as if you were the most important person in her life. But for all her beauty and loving ways, she has one major flaw.

Socs is stupid!

In a perceptive burst of ironic insight, our son Ken named her after history's most famous philosopher, but her sole contribution to the world so far has been to support the cat food industry with her vast powers of consumption. Intellectually, she ranks just below a mushroom; from her huge golden eyes shines the light of total confusion. The single sagacious act of her life was to con my wife into bringing her home, and it has been all downhill ever since.

But Socs does love my Lionel trains! Her expanded girth just barely allows her to squeeze through the tunnel portals, where she curls up in safety and comfort in the dark recesses beneath my hollow mountain and snoozes the day away.

Once I became aware of her tendency to block the main line in this manner, I developed the habit of evacuating the tunnel before running the trains. The method was simple; I called up my

Wabash GP-7 diesel from the marshaling yard and trundled it down to the portal, where its headlight illuminated the furry interloper. A light tap on the horn usually woke Socs instantly, whereupon she would stalk sleepily and indignantly to the center of my toy empire and proceed to take a bath amid my boxcars. At least this cleared the main line!

One day this necessary ritual slipped my mind. Fixated upon hauling the freight, I fired up that same Wabash diesel, hooked her to a half dozen tank and hopper cars, and with crew safely aboard the caboose we headed for the mountains. The locomotive slowly gained speed as she eased out of town, passed beneath a trestle and began the long descent into the valley. Through villages and pastures she thundered, until with a mighty blast of her horn she plunged into the tunnel.

Socs came out of that mountain like lava from Vesuvius, right through the top!

For a moment she was a feline Mt. Rushmore, a gargantuan black and white head amid the scattered pine trees and birches. Boulders cascaded down around her, buildings toppled, and the earth shook with her effort as she poised for one more thrust of her well-fed hindquarters. Like a suddenly freed champagne cork, Socs popped to freedom, crushing houses and barns and schools and parks beneath her prodigious paws during her terrifying descent from the summit. Like New York City after King Kong's pursuit of Fay Wray, ruin lay everywhere.

I wish I could report that Socs learned her lesson and avoided the railroad from thence and forever, but such is not reality: Socs is stupid! Whenever I forget to close the train room door, she is likely to curl up beneath my reconstructed mountain, and if I forget someday to clear the main line before the Limited streaks off to all points West, Mount Socrates may yet erupt once again!

Socrates, the tunnel-dwelling cat.

Featherweight Mountains the Easy Way

The secret to making strong but lightweight mountains in any configuration with a minimum of mess and a great saving in time is to be found in conventional 4' x 8' foam insulating sheets from a building supply house. These sheets may be purchased in various thicknesses; the ones I use most are 1, 2 and 4 inches. With a sharp kitchen knife I carve approximate shapes to simulate the contours of hills, valleys and riverbanks, stacking as many rows of foam as necessary to reach any desired height. Carpenter's glue holds them together firmly and permanently.

Once the general shape has been achieved and the glue is dry, it's easy to carve more subtle details into the foam. Then cracks are sealed with Poly-Filla or the crack-filling compound used for taping wallboard; this material may also be used to smooth out surfaces or to build up small terrain features.

If there are gaps too large to fill with the compound, such as around tunnel portals, small pieces of foam may be glued in place and then plastered over. When the overall design is satisfactory, sandpaper may be used to add final contours or to erase unwanted details. This texturing process can be as simple or as painstaking as the modeler wishes, but I have found that the foam provides a very convincing representation of many natural earth and rock shapes, without too much additional attention.

If the foam is broken rather than cut, a rough surface that resembles partially exposed boulders will result. Smooth cuts that are stacked in such a way that they do not meet adjacent layers evenly produce the appearance of quarried surfaces and ledges. Sanded surfaces will most closely approximate earth.

Sheets of foam insulation are easy to cut to the approximate shapes required for hills and rock faces. A sharp knife produces a fairly smooth surface, while breaking the foam gives a pebbly surface that resembles boulders.

By the time a mountain has been properly carved, the layout and most of the room will be filled with particles of foam. The largest will clog a vacuum cleaner, and should therefore be swept up before a general cleaning is done. This material is extremely light and clings to most surfaces by static electricity, so careful attention to this clean-up is recommended.

The final step is painting. I start with the tan base coat again, then add grass to horizontal surfaces wherever it would logically grow. The green coat may be added with a large brush and not worked in too heavily, if patches of earth are meant to show through. The surface of the foam accomplishes this effect naturally, as the bristles of the brush pass over small crevices.

Grass would not normally grow on vertical surfaces; nor would these be entirely the color of dirt, as soil cliffs would erode. A light brushing of gray paint with a stiff brush makes a convincing representation of cut or blasted stone, such as can be found where a hill has been cut away for a highway or rail line. Absolute realism is not the aim here; an impression of familiar scenery is. See color photo 33.

Carving and sandpapering shapes the foam into proper scenic details easily. The crack filler blends well with the foam but usually appears smoother, and may require roughening to match properly.

At this point any special inclusions in the scenery, such as roads climbing the mountains, can be painted to match the desired surface (brown or tan for dirt, gray for pavement). It is always easy to overpaint if mistakes are made, so great care is not essential. Latex paint is the best choice; it cleans up easily with soap and water, dries very quickly and has much less odor than oil-based paints.

Lakes and Rivers the Easy Way

In order to use my bridges in a convincing manner, I have included a lake and river in the layout, the former doubling as an access hatch to allow me to work on the interior areas. Realistic water can be achieved by a variety of means, and a survey of the back issues of *Model Railroader* and *Railroad Model Craftsman* will reveal artistic applications of such materials as casting resin.

Producing a convincing rippled surface is the key to good water, which is why regular glass and plastic are not effective.

The simplest solution I have found is available from the hardware store. Rectangular panels for recessed fluorescent light fixtures are available in many patterns, and one, a pebbly surface closely resembling wind-blown waves, makes great model water. It is easily cut and light in weight, and its gray color is close to the appearance of real water on an overcast day. (Despite the popular misconception, most rivers and lakes do not appear to be blue, except when strong light reflected from a sunny sky imparts that color.)

The plug for my combination lake and access hatch is a two-foot-wide section of foam, cut out in the center in a river-bank shape and glued to the plastic "water" of the lake. No special effects of shading have been employed, as the impression of water seems quite good. Those who are so inclined and have the time may wish to paint the plastic on its underside, lighter near the shore and darker at the center to simulate deeper water. The natural look shown here, however, is entirely appropriate for a toy train atmosphere. Note that it was unnecessary to cut the table top for this hatch, as the required space was left when the tables were assembled together.

While on this general subject, a quick survey of the bridges on my layout might be in order; they form an eclectic group. In addition to the 313 bascule bridge, I have two Marx truss designs, three ornate Standard Gauge Lionels and a couple of Postwar girder bridges. They are used to cross the water or to carry the passage of one track above another.

The rough surface of this fluorescent light fixture panel looks very much like wind-rippled water on a lake or river. The color is not unlike most Nova Scotia waterways on a cloudy day.

Elevated tracks are supported by Lionel's Postwar graduated trestle sets. These plastic erections are easy to install and fit securely between the ties of sectional and Gargraves track alike. I use them as Lionel did, without supports for the ties. While it may seem ludicrous for trains to be climbing on unsupported track, with nothing but ties and rails between the support columns, I have yet to have a visitor comment on this point. The effect, or impression, is satisfactory except on critical examination, and many a toy train layout in the past has sent its locomotives across such seemingly flimsy but actually quite secure trestles. Defying all logic, they look right.

Shrubs and Trees and Growing Things

Trees are essential to a convincing scene, especially in the rural areas. Many scale modelers claim you can never have too many, and fifty or a hundred will hardly seem enough if realism is intended. Unfortunately, they can be expensive to buy in such quantities, or very time consuming to manufacture at home. Again I refer you to the model magazines for a variety of suggestions, although my impressionistic solutions are far simpler than most of those, and fully satisfy the requirements of my toy empire.

Nova Scotia is filled with evergreen trees of every type. My yard contains numerous red and white pines, which in turn provide me with an unending supply of their likeness, in the form of pine cones. When inverted and sprayed green, they provide a convincing and persuasive interpretation of evergreens, at next to no cost or trouble. I collect them from the yard, drill small holes in the stems to accept thin finishing nails, fasten them to a piece of scrap lumber for painting, then insert them into the layout through pre-drilled holes.

Do they look exactly like pine trees? I guess not, but they do look like toy train trees, and much better to my eye than many of the lower-priced commercially available varieties. Of course, if price is no object and realism is the goal, there are excellent trees placed on the market by hobby manufacturers and architectural supply companies. I use a few of these to fill in, especially to represent the deciduous birches and maples so common here in the Maritimes. They aren't cheap, but they do look good.

Trees should also be varied in size, from shrubs to mature elms. The question of how many to plant is subject to personal taste. I like a clean look to a layout, with enough examples to suggest a scenic feature without interfering with the observation of other details. In short, too much forest obscures each tree! I have far too few to be a convincing representation of actual Nova Scotia countryside, but the overall impression is satisfactory.

While on the subject of quantity of detail, the most casual observation of the world around us reveals a surprising amount of clutter. Nowhere is this more apparent than in a railroad yard, and the best simulations as seen in the model press are loaded with such details. The average

Real Nova Scotia firs, spruces and pines provide their own replicas in the pine-cone evergreens spread throughout the author's layout. These miniatures are fast and easy to paint and install, and the price is right! The birch trees were supplied by an architectural models firm.

toy train layout, however, lacks these features. Perhaps the toy train world was meant to be more perfect than reality, for clean lines, open spaces and lack of garbage are characteristic of all those wonderful examples printed in the early Lionel catalogs. I wish my world were neater, too, so I make my railroad that way!

Providing for the Population

Where do the people live and work? I use a variety of sources for low-cost houses, stores and churches. They are neither highly detailed nor permanently attached to the table, and their yards contain only minimal detail: a path to the door, a few shrubs and trees, and the occasional hedge. The overall effect of a busy, lived-in town seems present, however.

Some structures were made from a book of Victorian cutout houses that were originally sold as a children's craft toy, and reprinted from an authentic copy. These are available in specialty gift shops or from Greenberg Publishing Company. They represent the same era as our earliest trains, and many details are printed in place, such as children and pets playing in yards, trees and shrubs, and impressions of pathways leading to the doors. The set includes a church, florist, blacksmith, photographer's shop, fire hall and numerous dwellings, all giving a pleasant antique appearance to the scene. The scale is appropriate for O Gauge layouts.

I also use wooden structures built from kits. Some (such as the engine house) have come from O scale suppliers, while others are the products of doll house manufacturers and convey the same turn-of-the-century flavor as the Victorian cutouts.

There are many structures of the Plasticville variety on the market, providing instant towns at relatively low cost. They suggest the 1950s, however, and to my eye they do not blend well with wood and paper structures, or with accessories from the 1920s and '30s; the plastic shine is jarring. But if used homogeneously and in large quantities, they make an excellent display for a Postwar layout.

Available in low-cost cutout books, these reprints of Victorian toy houses fit in well with the concept of toy trains from the early part of the century. They can be placed wherever needed on the layout, and are easily moved when a change is desired. Their printing suggests yards and pathways, and includes people and pets as well.

These wooden structures came in a Christmas village kit, produced by a dollhouse maker.

Details, Details, Details!

No layout is complete without at least some indication of life and activity within; people, animals and automobiles, and the little things like mailboxes, park benches and traffic signs all contribute to the overall atmosphere. One of the easiest ways to suggest the era of a layout is through the careful selection of model cars. Most people recognize a '30s-style automobile, or the Model-T profile that exemplifies the 'teens and early '20s. Cars form one of the most powerful identifiers of a time period, and examples of the correct size are available in toy and hobby shops and by mail order.

The model press carries advertisements from suppliers of everything from miniature people and pets to farm implements, livestock and bicycles, plus such exotica as amusement park rides and even complete circuses. Any theme is possible with a little imagination and some careful searching.

Cars and trucks are a quick reference point for those attempting to date a model railroad. These examples are representative of the 1930s, and fit in well with the overall impression created by the Lionel accessories and most of the trains that run on the author's layout. (The Lionel 442 diner was acquired after plans for this layout were completed, and it was subsequently shoehorned into the largest available empty lot in town. It does not appear on the track plan.)

Guiding the Viewer's Eye

The prudent modeler will attempt, by the location of scenic items, to draw the attention of the viewer to specific points of attraction. This can most easily be accomplished by using the principles of perspective which have been discussed throughout this book.

In general, depth is created artificially by locating slightly oversized structures and details nearest to the viewer, and placing smaller things to the rear. Undersized houses on distant mountaintops seem much farther away than they really are. City buildings in the foreground with two or more stories draw the eye, and add to the illusion of distance when compared with low-rise structures at the back.

The largest trains should be run on the nearest tracks (in this case, loops one and two that go under the mountain), and small ones (such as those Lionel Junior streamliners) stay on loops that serve the back forty acres. On routes that wind both near and far, mid-sized trains look best, such as Flying Yankees and those in-between American Flyer steamers.

The only large scenic items that may be placed far away are those that are expected to be on a big scale. We are so accustomed to huge power and microwave transmission towers on hilltops that the presence of Lionel's 394 beacon does not destroy the illusion of distance. However, large lamp posts should be positioned at the forward edge, and only shorter ones used near the faraway stations (which, by the way, should be tiny ones like the Lionel 137 or 48W).

A final means of guiding audience attention is the careful addition of lights. Each type or group of illuminated buildings or accessories on my layout is wired to a separate on-off switch, so that I may turn them on selectively as I orchestrate my glowing presentations. Each new glimmer in a darkened layout room attracts the eye to the next wonder about to unfold.

I am often asked how long it takes to build my creations. The average is about three months of spare time, excluding planning, to produce a layout. The following nine or ten months afford plenty of opportunity for operation and presentation to visitors, and by then I am bursting with new ideas and can't wait to tear up the track. Planning a new layout begins the same day as completion of the previous one.

This brings us to the end of our journey; the railroad is now complete, at least until I discover some new treasure from the past to add to its appeal. In both intent and execution, it represents the style and technology of generations past, my own personal and living museum. Perhaps I have struck a responsive chord within you; that was my intent.

If so, bring down those Trains from Grandfather's Attic!